Heart of Hearts

The Nature of Reality
And
How to Listen to Your Heart of Hearts
To Find True Peace, Joy and Love

Robert Shay

ISBN: 1-4392-3024-2
ISBN-13: 9781439230244

Visit www.booksurge.com to order additional copies.

Dedication

To Strife. For encouraging me to embrace my spiritual lessons and find the peace and joy we all seek.

To Donna
Namasté + Happy
Travels!

Love,
Bob

There are known knowns. These are things that you know you know. There are known unknowns. These are things that you know you don't know. There are also unknown unknowns. These are things that you don't know you don't know.

—Anonymous (paraphrased)

Contents

Introduction

When one sits down to write a book about spiritual enlightenment, which is what *Heart of Hearts* is about, it is not an endeavor that is planned. It is an endeavor that calls and draws itself forth from the writer. It becomes a vacuum that must be filled in much the way the quest for it began as an undeniable desire.

There are many of us today who have this desire, and we are seeking answers to age-old questions about why we exist and why we find ourselves to be alive and on earth at this exact moment, experiencing this life with these particular people. We want to understand our purpose on a deeper spiritual level. We feel impelled to learn about our ultimate reality. We are searching beyond the superficial duties of our day-to-day existence and looking for the deeper meaning.

We have achieved a level of comfort and wealth that is unprecedented, and "regular" people are experiencing disenchantment with traditional answers to these questions. With the advent of near universal education and the ability to read, learn and reason independently, a large number of people now have an ability to pursue these questions as never before in the history of the world.

We want more than a belief structure that tells us to "just believe" because that is what has always been done, even if these teachings have been "updated" by the institutions that promote them. We want answers that feel right, make sense and are "provable" to ourselves. We feel, as people have always felt, that there is more to understand and know and experience than the structure into which we have been indoctrinated. Now we have the ability, the education, the opportunity and the technology to pursue it on our own. And we are doing exactly that, in droves.

Those who are pursuing these answers may not realize it, but what they are looking for is spiritual enlightenment—a process of self-discovery that results in calm certitude about the answers to those questions. It is an inner knowing that proves valid every day and creates lasting peace drawn from the eternal, not the temporary.

Once activated, the quest for enlightenment can take on a life of its own with exactly the right people and information seeming to arrive at exactly the right moment to move the seeker to the next level of understanding. In this way the process becomes custom tailored to the individual and not only supports their search but becomes, in itself, a proof of its verity.

We are, as a global society of individuals, following our instinctive need to advance our spiritual understanding to the highest level possible with the tools at our disposal. We are no longer willing to believe something just because someone told us it is true. We have learned throughout history, and in our own short lives, that other people may not have our best interests at heart. Indeed, they may be preying on our desires and insecurities for their own worldly gain. We hear stories of religious cults, and we wonder if we have the ability to discern the truth.

We are still very willing to believe in higher powers, immortal realities and God, but we are beginning to require that our faith come with some kind of verification that we feel and know in our hearts is right and true. We can employ our intuition in this regard. We have the freedom to say "yes" to some ideas and pathways and "no" to others that do not support this forward movement because our quest is voluntary and deeply personal.

When we encounter "truth" we recognize it in our core. Thinking about it makes us happy and improves our life. New ideas that substantiate the concepts can be incorporated into our own personal theology to enhance our understanding and thus our lives; ideas that do not accomplish this objective may be discarded at our discretion.

We are all born with the ability to recognize whether any given person, action or spiritual path is good and true. In this book I call that ability our "heart of hearts." We can choose to listen to it and embrace our higher self, or we can ignore it and embrace our fearful self. The majority are still driven by their fearful self and afraid that they may get caught by that evil charlatan and led astray. Others hold fast to a teaching that threatens them with a fear of eternal punishment, and still others do not feel qualified to decide for themselves.

Those who decide to listen to their higher self are discovering a wealth of information on the topic of spiritual progress and many books, tapes, videos, seminars, retreats and groups. True offerings in this area are dedicated to creating a more peace-filled society by giving each individual the opportunity to show themselves that something as simple as a new way of thinking can produce noticeable benefits in their lives. These proofs are offered freely with no expectation of reward.

A dedication to the topic will reveal that the ideas are not new and in fact are the same across all areas of serious inquiry. These ideas are the core of all religions great and small, and every philosophical analysis lands at the same spot: the answers that you seek are found within. Quantum physics is inching toward this truth and ancient texts uncovered recently, such as the Gospel of Mary and the Gospel of Thomas (which were not included in the Bible), impart a message that we all contain the kingdom of God. They show a teaching of enlightenment rather than a teaching that pertains to our material reality.

There is only one top to the mountain, but there are a thousand pathways up. Whether you chose to acknowledge your ultimate reality through a rosary prayer, Buddhist meditation, the study of philosophy, the inspired creation of artistic beauty or simply communing with nature, you are accessing the same eternal truths.

Heart of Hearts is a brief review of these truths. This ancient yet still fresh way of thinking can add real value to your life. It is not an instruction manual for behavior. It seeks to help you learn to embrace inspiration so that you may act in ways that bring you closer to your Source. It uses examples drawn from everyday life to illustrate the concepts. It focuses on the gray rather than the black and white because it is in those gray areas of indecision that we all need the help we can receive from our heart of hearts.

In some places a masculine or feminine pronoun has been used to refer to the personification of ideas that clearly have no gender, such as God, Higher Self or Karma. It should not be assumed that this is anything more than a literary device that simply sounds better than the gender neutral pronoun "it."

Heart of Hearts makes the assumption that if you are ready for the messages contained herein, you are already an honest, faithful, moral, ethical, generally even-tempered spiritual seeker. It is also assumed that you are living a life that affords time for contemplation, not working day and night to put food on the table. Concerns of survival will tend to eclipse those of eternity, and these ideas will not find an eager audience among those who must fight simply to survive.

This is as it should be, for we are all moving along the same path but are on different points along it. The ultimate truth of what you are and where you are going is the same for everyone, and it always has been and always will be the same. Unlike the universe, it is eternal and unchanging, yet we are under no obligation to pursue it. We are drawn to it or we are not. If you feel inspired to learn about the topic, you can rest assured that it is the right thing for you to do. All are called, but few choose to listen. Eternity is in no hurry, however, and when you are ready it will be waiting.

This book will take you into concepts that may be unfamiliar, perplexing, difficult to understand and even wrong as far as your experience is concerned. It is my fervent hope however that you listen to the ideas and understand them on two levels, first with your mind then with your heart. As the light of understanding dawns on your awareness, reach into your heart of hearts and ask: Is this true? Does it feel right? Even if you disagree with the concept mentally, is there a portion of your being that doesn't disagree? Does that part of you need some time to digest the message because it suspects that after it does, it will agree?

The ideas are laid out in an easy-to-understand logical manner starting with our day-to-day reality and introducing the idea of instinctive behavioral habits. The spiritual concepts and their implications begin after that and build quickly on each other. The critical concept of who we really are and what we are all up against is explored early on and intentionally repeated and expanded upon throughout the entire book.

Your reward for successfully changing you mind about the nature of reality is true peace. It's the kind of peace that fills the hollow space in your gut; the kind that draws positive things into your life; the kind of peace that allows you to love truly and completely. When that happens, you feel joy.

Some of the modern masters who influenced this work are: Eckhart Tolle, Paramahansa Yogananda, Don Miguel Ruiz, Adyashante, David Hawkins, Timothy Freke, Jerry and Ester Hicks, Gary Renard, Byron Katie, Nouk Sanchez and Thomas Vieira, David Deida, Caroline Myss, Paulo Coelho, Gary Zukav, Brian Weiss, Robert Adams, James Redfield, Michael Newton, Robert Perry and Elsa Barker. By far the most influential ideas come from *A Course in Miracles*, and I am indebted to Dr. Kenneth Wapnick for his concise explanations of the true meaning of this master work.

This brings us back to the undeniable desire that formed the genesis of this book. Although it is presented and packaged as a lesson for anyone who cares to learn it, its higher purpose is personal.

Over many years of interest in the subject beginning with reading *Jonathon Livingston Seagull* as a young teen, my fascination has continued and grown over the past thirty-five years, in bursts and lulls, to the present where it has come to assume an increasingly important position in my life, becoming primary over the past five years.

The beauty of a journey such as this is that, far from removing one from life, it energizes every aspect as it draws positive energy and thus experiences and allows for the efficient removal of negative feelings and the internal strife they cause. This provides an opening to the power of inspiration that can pervade all areas of life if you allow it.

One result of this allowing is this book. In writing out the concepts that have become my constant companions and have enabled me to find real peace and joy, I have deepened my own understanding and moved further along my chosen path. If the ideas presented here help you to do this as well, I will rejoice with you and be glad that my words had a positive impact on your life.

Robert Shay
December, 2008

Chapter 1

Heart of Hearts

Your vision will become clear only when you look into your heart. Who looks outside, dreams. Who looks inside, awakens.

—Carl Jung

We all understand the idea of our heart of hearts. It means the real truth. Not the story we tell others or even ourselves. It means how we really feel and what we really know in our "heart of hearts."

We already know everything we need to know, but we have forgotten how to listen to ourselves. This is understandable. Our lives are busy, and our brains are shrill. In order to listen to our heart of hearts, we have to remember that we have one. Then we have to learn how to ask it questions. Then we have to learn to listen to the answers. It is no small task. It is fraught with uncertainty and mistakes. Although we all have the ability, just like everything worthwhile in our life, it takes practice.

Understanding and knowing that communion with yourself is not only real but possible will bring noticeable benefits to your life. It isn't necessary to become a mystic to achieve peace. Just being more honest with your self will help.

When someone asks you how you really feel, in your heart of hearts, they are asking you to tell them the truth as you might tell it to God, who already knows and cannot be fooled by anything you say or feel that is not authentic.

"In my heart of hearts, I know she just wants love and I know her anger and blame are not really directed at me."

"In my heart of hearts, I know this relationship isn't going anywhere and I'm just fooling myself by hoping it will change."

"In my heart of hearts, I admit that my religion/church/spiritual path doesn't fulfill me very deeply."

"In my heart of hearts, I know there is more to life than what I see and feel and have learned and experienced but I don't know what it is."

"In my heart of hearts, I know that I was once at peace but now it is more like a dream that I forgot a long time ago."

Chapter 2

Who Am I?

Now, here, you see, it takes all the running you can do, to keep in the same place. If you want to get somewhere else, you must run at least twice as fast as that.

—Lewis Carroll, *Through the Looking-Glass*

Robert Cialdini has written impressively about the psychology of influence and persuasion and in so doing explains some of the unconscious behavior patterns people use to cope with this complex task we call life. A surprisingly large number of our thoughts and actions are done from habit with little or no conscious thought. These "click whir" responses to situations allow us to navigate our day, and without them we would be paralyzed with indecision as we try to consciously examine all the possibilities. We have hundreds of rules we use, and unless someone points them out we aren't aware of them.

For instance, when we are unsure of what to do, most of us follow the crowd and do what everyone else is doing, such as standing and watching while someone chokes rather than rushing in to help.

The word "favor" immediately brings up an answer of "sure thing" even before we know the question.

The single word "because" is sufficient to initiate the "non-thinking habit" of compliance if it is easily performed. An example is when someone asks to cut in front of you in line *because* they are in a big hurry. If you are not in a big hurry, you will allow this 94 percent of the time. If they just ask to cut in line, you will allow it 60 percent of the time. If they ask to cut in line, *because* they want to cut in front of you in line, you will allow it 93 percent of the time. *(Influence, Robert Cialdini, 2001, p.4)*

We will do the most uncharacteristic things to be "liked" by someone whose opinion *of us* we value.

We don't think about these things. We just do them. We have even learned how to stop thinking about the task of driving the car and frequently arrive at our destination with little or no memory of actually driving there. In this way, we cope with the myriad small decisions and activities that life throws at us every day. The benefit, along with being able to navigate existence in the first place, is that we conserve our mental processing power so we can concentrate on the important things, like who might win the game tonight or if my partner loves me.

We are so busy doing things all day every day that unless something dramatic happens that rocks our foundation, we don't question very much at all. We get up every morning and go to school or work and raise the kids and take a vacation and have a party and look for our soul mate and worry and get angry and laugh and cry, and sometimes we try to find meaning.

And we do want meaning. We look for it everywhere. We want to have meaningful work and meaningful relationships. We want the act of raising children to be a meaningful activity. We go to church to seek spiritual understandings that give meaning to our lives.

If we get fired or divorced or our kid gets in trouble or tragedy strikes suddenly, that meaningful house of cards we have so carefully assembled can collapse, either entirely or partially, and we may find that we are lost. We realize that the peace we found was a false shadow of the real thing, or the love we thought was true has gone and may never return. Now what should we do?

Most begin rebuilding the house of cards. They blame other people and events or even themselves for their situation and think that the next time will be different. They promise themselves that they won't make the same mistakes. But we all do make the same mistakes, and the reason is because we haven't learned anything real. We continue to believe that the world can solve our problems if only _____ (you fill in the blank).

Maybe the world doesn't have the answers. Maybe answers aren't outside of you, and that's why when you look there you don't find true peace. Maybe everything you need to be happy and fulfilled is right there inside you, but you don't know how to look or how to access that part of your spiritual heritage.

We spend a lot of our time looking outward for solutions to our problems. Sometimes these solutions seem to solve the problem and are the right thing to do. Ending conflict with another person is certainly an outward-facing issue that should be addressed externally. If we don't include the inner self in our resolution, however, we are going to suffer a repeat of the same issue at a later date with a different person. Certainly you found this book and are reading it "out there," but if you don't "in"ternalize the message you are just reviewing words, and you will not gain the benefit.

If we want to fill the void we feel deep down and truly release ourselves from guilt and fear, there is only one way. It starts with an understanding of who we *really* are. Not who we think we are or who we profess to be or pretend to be or aspire to be, or even who we act like and speak like in our daily discourse. The journey isn't about who you are "out there." It's about who you are "in here." Without a clear understanding of *what* you are, you cannot put the concepts that will follow into the proper perspective and gain the very real value that they can bring to your life.

It is important to realize that the ideas that follow do not require you to change anything that you do "out there." You cannot affect the inner self by making changes to the outer, and you do not have to make any changes externally as you come to understand the inner condition. You will still go to work or school and search for love and talk to your friends and send flowers to your mother on her birthday. Nothing external will seem to change, and nothing needs to be changed by you in your life. If it needs to change, it will change of its own accord, in its own time, in direct proportion to the internal change you achieve.

The internal changes I am discussing apply to the way you think and about what you think. They are fundamental. They are the foundation from which all else arises. You have a foundation now, and everything that happens in your life arises from it. If you are not satisfied or fulfilled with your life, you can shift your foundation to one from which true joy can arise. It's like digging a well where there is no water. After many years of digging, you will eventually hit bedrock and that certainly won't quench your thirst!

Move the equipment to a new location, however, and beautiful clear cool water flows forth in abundance—more than enough for you and everyone you know. When you begin to understand your inner self, the well is found and can be tapped for the benefit of all who choose to drink. As your understanding changes and your inner reality assumes its proper place in your life, your outer reality will naturally follow. You find peace first, then your world becomes peaceful, not the other way around. You knew this, didn't you?

Chapter 3

Who Am I, Really?

Greater is He that is in you, than he that is in the world.

—I John 4:4

Before we address who, or more precisely *what*, you are, let's talk a little about what you might think you are. We'll do it with a series of questions. I'll ask and you answer. Go ahead and do this now while you are reading. Then I'll presume your answers and reply. Ready?

Are you your body?

Most people would say no. I inhabit my body, but "I" am not my body. Good answer. Almost everyone agrees that the body is a vehicle that allows "you" to experience life on planet earth. Even our language supports this conclusion. We say I *have* a body. We do not say I *am* a body. When it is old and tired and used up, "you" lay it down and "you" move on. We also call ourselves human beings. That means that we are a being who is currently human. Right? Okay, here's the next one.

Are you your thoughts?

You are thinking that since you aren't your body you must be your thoughts because they are with you constantly and help you make sense of everything. You kind of think that yes, you are your thoughts, but then you think that might not be right so you are going to say: "No, I am not my thoughts." But you aren't sure why.

Okay, is that your final answer? Good job. Right again. “You” are not your thoughts either.

What are thoughts anyway? Thoughts by and large are a physical construct and the result of the operation of a very important organ in your body, your brain. In the same way that your liver is designed to remove toxins and your heart is designed to pump blood, your brain is designed to, among other duties, think. Scientists have studied how this happens on a physical level and can tell us all kinds of things about synapses and electrochemical or enzymatic reactions to stimuli that produce the result we call thinking. Just like your liver, you have no conscious control over what your brain does to keep your body functioning, and like your heart you have a little bit of conscious ability to change the speed of the beats or in this case to direct your conscious thoughts. Thank goodness for the frontal lobe. If it weren’t there, you couldn’t read this book!

I don’t think that anyone is going to argue that the real “you” is the frontal lobe of your brain. Even if it is a very well-designed frontal lobe that gives its owner the ability to understand all kinds of abstract concepts and make connections that are beyond the reach of most, we still “know” that isn’t who we really are. We know this because we unconsciously reached inside and asked our heart of hearts, and it bubbled up an answer, albeit a subtle one, that we heard. In other words, we know intuitively that we are more than the sum of our thoughts, no matter how “intelligent” they are.

After all “we” are directing our thoughts. We turned them on the problem, we employed them to find an answer, and we arrived at a solution. Our thoughts didn’t do that on their own. They were used by us to accomplish a task. It is even possible to step back and watch (or listen to) your thoughts. You do it all the time but you aren't aware of it. "You" can have a debate with "yourself." "You" can be mad at "yourself." Language supports us as we say I *have* thoughts, not I *am* thoughts. Right?

Okay, so we are not our bodies, and we are not our thoughts. Ready for the next question?

Are you your soul?

Think about this one before your rush in and say yes. Anything that "you" *have* is not "you." How could it be? The real "you" has (i.e., possesses) this thing called a soul just like it has a body and a brain and thoughts; and a house and a car and a job. Right? You cannot *be* something that you have.

So let's talk about your soul. What is it? The common belief is that your soul is the part of you that, although present in the body, stays with you after the body's demise and contains "you" after death. Since it is present in the body and it contains you, "you" are at least once removed from your body. Your soul may very well have powers and abilities far beyond those of mortal man, but it is still not "you." You kind know this, but it's not the no-brainer the other two questions were.

So if you aren't your soul, what exactly are you?

Words, which are really "symbols of symbols"[1] begin to fail us at this point, but we can still move forward a little. If we follow the logic, we realize that the only thing we can say with

[1]Words are sounds that we make in our throat or markings on a page that represent ideas. As such they are symbols. The idea itself is also a symbol because the *idea* of something is not the thing itself. Therefore words are symbols of symbols. It is the best we have, and it works fairly well, but it should not be presumed to be more than an imperfect way of delivering a message from one person to another.

certainty is that "you" are the Awareness that is watching and experiencing your "life." We may not know anything beyond that, but we do *know* that we are aware! *I am*. I exist. I am aware of that. But who, or what, are we aware of and *who* is aware? We are aware of our being-ness; our consciousness; our existence. We are aware that we "are." Since we are "aware" of our being-ness, Awareness includes being-ness and consciousness. The real "you" is the Awareness that watches and is conscious of all that is.

For this reason Awareness is also referred to as the Watcher or the Observer or the Presence. It is the ultimate Experiencer of Experiences. Although Awareness is referred to by these and other names, it is really beyond them. The Observer or Author of your life exists within your Awareness. "Awareness" is also sometimes used to refer to your Higher Self. Everything exists within our Awareness and we can sense this Awareness, although we cannot understand it or become any more than conscious of its existence. The Awareness that is "us" is not accessible in the same way that we see and understand things in the world. Awareness sees, but cannot be seen.

We can catch a glimpse of our (Higher) Self when we look at our life from outside of it. You can step back and watch yourself go by. When you do this, "you" are looking at you from a place beyond that concept we all have of "our self." In other words we are looking from the perspective of our higher "Self" at our day-to-day "self." We don't do it consciously as much as we "catch" ourselves doing it. It happens when you are being honest with yourself or when "you" spot trends in "your" life. Who is spotting those trends? Who is being honest?

Unlike your body, your Awareness has no thoughts. How could it? It doesn't have a brain. Without a brain or thoughts, the

Watcher of your life has no agenda. It is not afraid because it is also "aware" of its immortal nature. It cannot make judgments because it has nothing that contrasts with its reality. Awareness (the real "you") cannot suffer any guilt or remorse because it doesn't have the same investment in "life" that you do. It is merely conscious of it.

Compared to our body, our soul might be thought of as immortal, but it is Awareness that really "has" a soul. When you speak of "your soul," you are speaking from an immortal perspective beyond it. In other words you are speaking as "Awareness."

Your Awareness/Higher Self is peaceful, and when you calm your mind you can perceive this peace if you try. It is a part of you, and it is quiet compared to the noise of the world, i.e., your brain's thoughts or emotions, or other people or events.

Your Higher Self is not your day-to-day consciousness or self. That is your ego, and we'll discuss this in the next chapter. Awareness is your heart of hearts, but it is more than that. It is the ultimate Observer. You can access the Observer (of which you are "aware") by moving your perspective back one step in your mind and consciously watching yourself from a place of detachment. Doing this is not only possible, it is beneficial because you are moving closer to your ultimate Self, which is the same thing as moving closer to God. People who have a close relationship with God embody the traits we have just described as belonging to Awareness.

When the Observer or Watcher or Author of our life is stripped away, Awareness yet remains, simply and completely "aware" of its existence.

Quiet though it may be, your Awareness is communicating with you constantly and is available for consultation. When you access your heart of hearts, you are tapping into Awareness, also known as your Higher or Greater Self. Most of us don't do this regularly, and when we do, it may not be very honestly, but we all "know" our heart of hearts is there and available if we choose to consult it.

People say things "happen for a reason" to describe events that seem to have no logical explanation or where the reason is not apparent. This thought subconsciously supports the idea that we are not in control and are, to some extent, victims of a plan beyond our perception. This leads us to hope that things will work out well because we know events could go against our "best laid plans."

We also experience coincidences that defy explanation. We have all received a call from a friend with whom we have not spoken or even thought about for years within a day or a couple weeks of thinking of them. Sometimes activities, either positive or negative, "conspire" in our life, which result in an outcome that seems should not be happening, as completely unrelated events come together at exactly the right time. We all know people with unnaturally good luck just like we know people with perennially bad luck. We toss it off to fate or karma and wish we had more of the good luck and hope to avoid the bad kind. Either way we are admitting that there are forces directing our lives that, try as we might, we cannot control. In the end we attribute them to God.

But it isn't God who is directing things. It's "you." You are authoring your existence by embracing fear (your day-to-day self) or trust (your Higher Self). Based on which "self" you choose, your life will improve or deteriorate. There are many reasons for this, and together we will explore some of them in later chapters of the book. We will also discuss how to "think" with an awareness of your Higher Self so that you can take advantage of this effect.

Becoming aware of your Awareness is the first step in understanding that the real "you" should be thought of as a Decision Maker who "decided" to become "aware" and have a little experience. You know this experience as your (so-called) life. When you are "in touch" with your Awareness of your consciousness, you are touching an eternal part of yourself that is aware of your true heritage beyond your day-to-day existence. You are stepping back from life as you know it and looking at things from outside, rather than inside. Life improves when you do this. Peace may come to you as a result. You might feel happier for no "reason" you can determine. If you continue thinking about this and try to look at the world as if you were Awareness (and not you), events will begin to conspire to keep you moving in this direction. It feels wonderful. This is the beginning of awakening to your true reality.

> The beginning of freedom is the realization that you are not "the thinker." The moment you start watching the thinker a higher level of thought becomes activated. You then begin to realize that there is a vast realm of intelligence beyond thought, that thought is only a tiny aspect of that intelligence. You also realize that all the things that truly matter—beauty, love, creativity, joy, inner peace—arise from beyond the mind. You begin to awaken.
>
> —Eckhart Tolle

When you have a dream at night, it is obvious that you (your subconscious mind) created the whole thing. You thought it up in all of its outlandish reality. Every symbolic character and surreal place came from inside you. That makes everything in your dream part of you. It cannot be anything else.

If the real "you" is the Decision Maker who decided to "create" an experience called life, just as your brain "creates" the experience of your dreams, it means that this Decision Maker is having an experience (your life) that is on the same level of reality to it as your dreams are to you. In this reality we call life, that your true self "dreamed," you may be all powerful, or a victim of circumstances, just as you are in your dreams. It doesn't matter which. Both are equally "unreal" to the Maker of the Dream. They are just experiences. "You" will wake up from the dream called life and embrace your true reality in the same way that you wake up from your dreams in the morning. It is just a matter of when.

As long as the "dream of life" continues, however, it means that everything that is part of your Awareness is part of "you." It can't be anything else.

Sometimes when you are dreaming, you become aware that you are dreaming as you are doing it. This is called lucid dreaming. You realize with your conscious mind that you are dreaming. Suddenly it's not real to you anymore, it's just a dream. You could begin directing the action if you wanted—being the all-powerful creator of the dream—or you could decide to wake up.

When you wake up to your eternal reality as the Decision (Dream) Maker who decided to have an experience, it is kind of like waking up in the morning from a dream. Suddenly the consequences of events in the world or your life don't seem as stressful as they did. The "dream of life" continues, of course, but your perspective changes. We'll explore our Decision Maker a little later in the book and learn how we can begin to *live* with a conscious understanding of our true reality as Awareness.

> When I look inside and I see that I am nothing (Awareness could easily be classified as "no-thing"), that is Wisdom. When I look outside and realize that I am everything that is Love.
>
> —Sri Nisargadatta Maharaj

Here in the world, you and I are clearly different people leading similar but separate lives. We have separate experiences and beliefs, different bodies and abilities, different attitudes and aspirations. We can't deny this, but it only makes sense on the level of our bodies and our thoughts and our shared belief in a common "reality" we call life.

Your permanent identity as the Decision Maker, however, is not different, *in any way* from my permanent identity, which is also the Decision Maker. In this respect we are identical. In other words, we are one Consciousness that is having multiple experiences *and* we are everything our Awareness perceives. Therefore, we are one with the universe and everything in it. Wow.

We can conclude that it is probably a good idea to get in touch with our inner Awareness as we wonder why in the world things would be set up this way.

It can also lead to fear if we think that our separate self isn't "real" and neither is the world and everything in it. If it isn't real, why do we perceive ourselves to be here? What is the point, and what is our real purpose?

This little exercise does not mean we are not living life here in the world. Of course we are. It would be silly to think we are not. The world and our lives cannot be denied. This explanation of who you are (as your ultimate reality) will allow you to begin to expand your understanding to include a concept of yourself that is much greater than you currently perceive it to be. Your Decision Maker is timeless and immortal, and that is who *you* are at your essential core. You think you are a person living in the world and you are certainly that. You are also a lot more than that.

Your life here does have meaning, and you are living it for a reason. Your triumphs and pleasures, your disappointments and defeats serve a purpose. The purpose is to bring you closer to your true reality. Allow yourself to embrace that feeling of

Awareness-of-being and use it as a bridge to get in touch with your immortal Self. If you begin to think about your life from that perspective, you will begin to find real meaning, as trials become opportunities to accomplish your purpose and joy is your reward.

Give yourself permission to imagine that your real reason for being is to live a life that brings you closer to your Self as that Decision Maker. It is the only purpose that has eternal significance. Everything else is transient and temporary, and the meaning is impossible to place in a greater context. You give up on the task every day as you admit that you don't know why things happen and you fail to find real meaning in anything. You react more on instinct and habit than with a conscious understanding of who you are, where you are going and why.

You are the Decision Maker. Your life is designed to help you understand this so you can wake up to your immortal reality as one with God and all that is. The reason you want to do that now is because it reduces stress, improves your health, and brings peace and joy into your life. As you move closer to your real Self, you feel better and your "life" here in the world improves. When you move away, your life becomes more uncomfortable and difficult. It's as simple as that. When you embrace your best immortal qualities like kindness, compassion, humility and love, you are embracing your Higher Self. When you engage in harm to others, anger, jealousy, suspicion or hate, you are embracing your fearful self, also called the ego. We will explore the characteristics of the ego in upcoming chapters.

Throughout the rest of the book, I will refer to life as a dream or an illusion because as far as Awareness is concerned that's what it is. Awareness of your being-ness is a stepping stone to realizing that you are the Decision Maker who decided to have this dream (for a reason we'll discuss later), but that decision in no way effects who you are in the eternal sense.

This does not mean that you should decide that life doesn't matter because you are just dreaming and you're not really here. That's not the lesson at all. You are here because you are not in touch with your Awareness, much less your Decision Maker, and you will not become connected to it overnight. Realizing, in the deepest core of your being, that you are not separate from anyone or anything (even God) is the purpose of your life.

The Decision Maker is not an aspect of our Self that we can truly embrace. We may be "aware" of our consciousness, and see our self from the perspective of the Watcher and feel the Presence that is our Self, but we are *not* aware of the Decision Maker. Simply knowing that there is a Decision Maker is all that is necessary here in the world of form.

Our time here is filled with opportunities that we can take advantage of to move closer to our true Self (as the one who made this decision), if we can see them for what they are. The purpose of this book is to help you identify and understand these opportunities within the framework of moving closer to your Self as one with all that is. You can do it if you choose. You don't have to do it, but your life will improve if you do. You will begin to see the real meaning in everything. It will all start to make sense in a "larger perspective" kind of way.

Just like everything worthwhile, it is not easy. There are trials and obstacles to be overcome, but they would be there anyway. The purpose of your ego is to prevent you from learning anything about your Self as the Decision Maker, and it is the ego that is using life's difficulties to keep you unaware.

> You recognize from your own experience that what you see in dreams you think is real while you are asleep. Yet the instant you waken you realize that everything that seemed to happen in the dream did not happen at all. You do not think this strange, even though all the laws of what you awaken to were violated while you slept. Is it not possible that you merely shifted from one dream to another, without really waking?
>
> —*A Course in Miracles* T10.I.23–6

Chapter 4

Ego

> *Within this kingdom the ego rules and cruelly... This fragment of your mind is such a tiny part of it that, could you but appreciate the whole, you would see instantly that it is like the smallest sunbeam to the sun, or the faintest ripple to the ocean. In its amazing arrogance, this tiny sunbeam has decided it is the sun; this almost imperceptible ripple hails itself as the ocean... Yet neither the sun nor ocean is even aware of all the strange and meaningless activity.*
>
> —*A Course in Miracles* T-18. VIII.3:1, 3:4, 4:1

Every person on the planet has a running dialog going on inside their heads all the time. We talk to ourselves 24/7. If we verbalized that dialog, we might not be allowed out in public unsupervised. Even at night the dialog continues as we sleep (in dreams) and only the greatest of mystics can claim to be able to stop thought for any length of time.

So to whom or what are we talking and listening? Is this Awareness? Is this how we tap into and control our destiny and our fortune? The answer is no and yes.

No, it is not Awareness, because Awareness doesn't "talk"; and yes, this is how our destiny and our fortune is determined here in this illusion we call reality. Although we manifest or author our existence, we have little conscious control over the outcome. It is mostly unconscious, and that's how our ego wants it.

If our mind is an iceberg, our day-to-day conscious mind is the tip. Most of what we think and feel is subconscious.

Getting consciously in touch with your subconscious is almost an oxymoron. Yet this is where our true power to affect our destiny is located.

Let's look at our conscious thoughts and examine that dialog. Ninety percent of the time the "thing" we are talking to is our ego. Imagine a little devil sitting on your shoulder whispering in your ear. The other ten percent is your Awareness; but it doesn't "talk," remember? It's just aware. You have accessed Awareness when you just "know" something is right (or wrong) but you can't say why. Awareness is working through you when you feel inspired or experience love or appreciation or harmony with all things.

Your ego has a vested interest in preventing you from listening to or even knowing about your awareness of any form of your Higher Self, because if you knew about that, you might realize that "you" decided to be here and "you" could change your mind, and that would be the end of the ego. Oh, that it were only so easy. It isn't. Your ego is deeply ingrained in you and rising above it is not as simple as making a conscious decision to do so.

The ego pretends to be "you" when it whispers in your head and you accept that it is "you" who is talking to "yourself." In this way you are essentially controlled by your ego. We all have one, and it is responsible for all the misery and the short-lived happiness in this world of form. The sweet nothings it whispers have a profound effect on your life. Judgment and suspicion are ego attributes. So are guilt, anger, hatred, jealousy and resentment to name just a few.

These thoughts generate fear and drive behavior. They create issues and problems that take up most of our conscious thoughts and time. Sometimes they produce the desired result, and the person gets what they always wanted—the money, the house, the power or the girl or the guy. The hallmark of an ego success, however, is that it soon feels hollow and is short lived. It never satisfies. Quite the opposite. It merely increases the desire for more and perpetuates the cycle. Think of an alcoholic.

> Matter gave birth to a passion that has no equal, which proceeded from something contrary to nature. Then there arises a disturbance in its whole body.
>
> —*The Gospel According to Mary Magdalene*

The ego never gives anything except something that has no value to it, and then it wants something of value in return. This describes most of our "relationships." We give something that we do not value (ourselves) and take something we think has value (the other person). The ego tricks you into believing that the empty feeling inside can be filled with some *one* from the outside.

Relationships are a wonderful case in point. As a species we have almost no understanding of the real dynamics. We have been brainwashed into believing that love conquers all and that fleeting feeling will carry us into bliss for eternity. That isn't how it usually works except in the movies.

This is what happens in a "love" relationship. Two people meet and an attraction develops. They communicate with words and gestures and inflection and humor and pheromones and eye contact, but they don't actually "see" the other person. They see a projection of what their ego wants the other person to be. They see an idealized version based on someone else they know very well and love deeply, like a parent or a sibling or even the imagined qualities of the boy or girl who got away. All the while their ego is hiding their "real selves" and revealing only their most interesting and attractive qualities.

This early dance to avoid revealing our true selves may result in a phenomena known in this world as "love." Our eyes glaze over as we imagine that maybe, just maybe, we have found someone who will actually accept our ego's "gift" of ourselves and return to us something we can really use, like self-respect or happiness, and if that's not possible, at least money or creature comforts. In the words of *A Course in Miracles*, we are "giving to get" and it is a hallmark of the ego.

It is possible to have a long relationship with another person under the ego's direction that provides enough satisfaction and meets enough needs to keep the couple together, but as with all things ego, it feels hollow and is void of real meaning. Both people have merely compromised their ideals and resigned themselves to living together in a symbiotic existence that covers their most basic needs and provides minimal and fleeting moments of happiness or peace. This is the intention of the ego, and it is known as a Special Relationship.

Special Relationships are not limited to love relationships, but are present in every significant relationship we have with other people. These are not the only kind of Special Relationships we have, either. Any relationship we have with an activity, like a job, and our relationships with things, like cars or computers, and even our relationship with ourselves are all forms of Special Relationships.

> Special Love and Special Hate Relationships are the same. Both are based on scarcity, selfishness and greed. They are the ego's way of giving us something unreal to try to fill the void created by separation. Special Love always turns to Special Hate and this keeps the mind preoccupied with the separated world. Special Love distracts you from unconscious feelings of self loathing so you do not feel its pain. However, since it is impossible to love someone you see as fundamentally separate from yourself this does not last long. When they can no longer distract you, Special Love turns to Special Hate where we project our unconscious guilt onto our partner.
>
> —Ken Wapnick

The ego is very consistent with its message that the problem is "out there" with the other person or external event and you are not at fault. Even when you admit fault, there is usually a very good reason like you were overtired or stressed. The ego will lie to save face rather than admit the truth.

You can admit, in your heart of hearts, that you always think that if you could just find someone who understood you, or you got that raise or promotion or house or car or golf score or your kid cleaned up his act or your spouse was more affectionate, that *you* could be happy and find peace. We all make this mistake. We listen to our ego. It is very insistent and persuasive. Blame is one of its chief weapons. So are survival and fear of death.

Contrast this to Awareness. Our Higher Self has no fear. Joy is its overarching attitude and true peace is its disposition. As the Decision Maker, we actually exist in a state of bliss, also known as Love, which springs forth from eternity and permeates all. The problem is that we are many levels removed from this bliss. The ego keeps us distracted with external events and people, and in so doing it hopes we will never learn of our true heritage and will continue searching for satisfaction in the world.

If the ego renders the good times hollow and revels in our pain, what are those good feelings that we sometimes experience? What are the love and joy and peace that we feel in life? Are these not true? They feel pretty good.

The love and peace and happiness that we feel are authentic, but they are shadows of the real thing. The love of a mother for her child, the peace that can be found through selfless acts of service, and the joy that exists in a job well done are very real. They are fleeting, however. The mother can become exasperated with her child, the futility of your charity may take away from its charm, and happiness at achievement never seems to last no matter how true it seems. Sooner or later the ego manages to snatch success from the arms of victory and that little voice begins to undermine your greatest accomplishments. The feelings can be best understood as a glimpse into the real thing. If you like how they feel for the short time they are around, you will love the eternal version you can find inside yourself.

For all the terrible thoughts it has and all the mayhem they cause, the ego is not our enemy. It is us, too, and without it we would not exist as separate beings. The ego is our resistance to truth, our belief that the dream is real and has meaning, in and of itself.

Let's look at an example of the ego at work from a seemingly unlikely place, a church. In the January 18, 2008, edition of the *Wall Street Journal* we find an article entitled, "Banned From Church." An excerpt:

> On a quiet Sunday morning in June, as worshippers settled into the pews at Allen Baptist Church in southwestern Michigan, Pastor Jason Burrick grabbed his cell phone and dialed 911. When a dispatcher answered, the preacher said a former congregant was in the sanctuary. "And we need to, um, have her out A.S.A.P."
>
> Half an hour later, 71-year-old Karolyn Caskey, a church member for nearly 50 years, who had taught Sunday school and regularly donated 10 percent of her pension, was led out by a state trooper and a county sheriff's officer. One held her purse and Bible. The other put her in handcuffs.
>
> The charge was trespassing, but Mrs. Caskey's real offense, in her pastor's view, was spiritual. Several months earlier, when she had questioned his authority, he'd charged her

> with spreading "a spirit of cancer and discord" and expelled her from the congregation. "I've been shunned," she says.
>
> Her story reflects a growing movement among some conservative Protestant pastors to bring back church discipline, an ancient practice in which suspected sinners are privately confronted and then publicly castigated and excommunicated if they refuse to repent. While many Christians find such practices outdated, pastors in large and small churches across the country are expelling members for offenses ranging from adultery and theft to gossiping, skipping service and criticizing church leaders.

The minister in this story is not to blame for listening to his ego. He does not realize that he has one, beyond the Freudian version. He thinks his ego *is* him. He believes the feelings his ego engenders are real because he believes we are bodies and souls. He may repent and ask forgiveness and wonder why he struggles so hard to release his angry feelings.

When you are talking to someone, you are talking to their ego. You communicate to and with Awareness when you are in touch with and project positive *feelings* like empathy, tranquility, kindness and compassion. We share one Awareness as far as our eternal reality is concerned but we do not share one ego. The ego is our belief in separation from everyone and everything and we are not one with other egos. The ego cannot perceive the concept of oneness and that means we have difficulty understanding it too. The ego is our day-to-day mind. Awareness comes to us as deep feelings that we know intuitively are true.

The best way to start to recognize your ego and overcome it in your mind is to refer to it in the third person. "My ego doesn't like messiness." "My ego is angry!" "My ego is jealous." Even positive feelings can be ego driven and overcome in the same way. "My ego is happy I got that promotion." "My ego is enthusiastic." "My ego enjoyed that meal." "My ego forgives you."

Your Greater Self has none of these kinds of feelings because they are of the world and are temporary. "You" are eternal and unchanging, just like God. When you feel peace because you touched your true Self, and sensed your connection to God, that is a positive feeling that came from your Awareness. When you feel peace and can finally relax after finishing a big project, that kind of peace is from your ego. When you are happy just to be alive and you feel your connection to nature, that happiness springs from your Awareness of the fact that everything is one. When you are happy because you learned that somebody loves you, that happiness came from the ego. When you give comfort or a smile or assistance when it is needed and truly want nothing in return, the positive feelings that result came from your Higher Self. Gratitude because someone helped you out of a jam is of the ego. Gratitude because you now understand that you have an eternal reality beyond your day-to-day existence is of your Higher Self.

When you feel inspiration and creativity, those feelings are coming from your Higher Self, too. The ego cannot participate because it does not recognize anything that is not of the world. The ego will certainly enjoy the feeling of accomplishment the creativity produced and try to take credit for the outcome. Most creative people will give the credit to inspiration and take little for themselves or their ego. They just know that the reason the project went well and they are the recipient of accolades is because it was encouraged by a higher power beyond them.

The ego is with us always, and we will never release it while we are of this world. We can recognize its behavior, however, and that is just as effective. Until now the ego has been hidden. Now it is exposed and we can begin to see the many tricks it uses to keep our attention pointed outward and prevent us from learning the truth of who we really are. There is much to follow on the ego and its subtle traps. As you learn to detect them, the ego becomes more an inconvenience than a threat. Eventually it becomes an assistant because it points to areas of release that we must overcome in our quest to achieve our immortal reality.

> If you bring forth what is within you, what you bring forth will save you. If you do not bring forth what is within you, what you do not bring forth will destroy you.
>
> —Gospel of St. Thomas

Chapter 5

Now

The past is history
The future is a mystery
Today is a gift
And that's why it is called
The Present.

Let's talk a little about time. The past, the present and the future are abstract notions that are necessary to operate here in the physical world. Our society would not have progressed if we could not learn from our mistakes and plan for the future. The concept of time is an essential concept for our survival.

The past and the future are not "real," however. The past is a memory trace and the future hasn't happened yet, so how could they be real in any sense of the word? Maybe some past action "was" real or a future action is "going to be" real, but they aren't real now. When they are real, that time was or will be "now."

The only thing that is real is what is happening right this second.

Your Higher Self doesn't worry about the future nor does it ruminate about the past. It is merely "aware" of the here and now, which is the only real time. In your Higher Self's awareness, the past, present and future are all the same thing. The future has already happened, the past can be relived, and all of it can occur right now.

Time is a concept that is necessary in the physical universe. Take away the universe and you remove the need for time. In the absence of a physical place, time is holographic, meaning that everything exists at once. It is merely a matter of where you put your attention, or, in this discussion, your Awareness.

In your dreams you don't stop to check your watch. You don't worry about what happened or plan for the future. You are on a wacky roller-coaster experience, and you just absorb everything that is happening. If you have a question about what just happened, you rewind and relive it. If you are curious about how something will turn out, you can fast forward to the end. In other words you move everything into the present in order to experience it in the only time there is, right now.

This is how Awareness experiences your life. *You* have to experience it in a linear fashion because you don't have the ability to move time around within the dream of life. One of the best ways to connect with your Higher Self is to do what it does and live in the moment.

When you live in the moment you pay much greater attention to what you are doing or thinking or feeling right now. You block worries about the future, stop mulling over the past, and just experience washing your hands or walking up the steps. You train all your attention on the activity, experience it without any judgment, and use only as much thought as is necessary to accomplish the task. If you are sitting in a chair relaxing after a long day, try noticing the texture of the fabric under your hands instead of thinking about a problem at work. Give your mind a rest and be in the moment. Do it by noticing little things that you never paid attention to before. Your mind could use the rest, and you can connect with your Self by mirroring its natural state as an Experiencer of experiences and examining the "unimportant" details. It's a nice time out. When you move to the next thing, you'll be refreshed and your thoughts will be clearer. If you spend every spare second rehashing the same old worry thoughts, you will be tired and have trouble concentrating.

Have you ever "spaced out"? Just sat there and stared into space and had no thoughts? Everyone does it. It usually only lasts a couple seconds. When you notice, you shake yourself out of it and get back to thinking with a "now where was I?" thought as if you shouldn't be allowing your brain to stop like that. You just stepped out of time—again.

Spacing out with no thought is a very good thing to do. If you can, you should do more of it, not less. For a second or so you are communing with your Awareness by mirroring its empty vessel. If you are going to receive inspiration, which is one of the ways your Higher Self communicates, you must be receptive. You aren't receptive if your (ego) thoughts are taking all of your attention.

Eckhart Tolle has a wonderful technique for stopping thought temporarily. Sit quietly and allow yourself to relax and let your mind drift. Begin to slowly focus in on your thoughts and "watch" them happen. You might hear yourself thinking about your upcoming weekend or worrying about your bills. As you watch your thoughts in this manner, pose this question: "I wonder what thought will come next?" This will have the effect of stopping the next thought for a moment or two as you wait and listen for that next thought. Try it right now. It works. There you have it. A gap in your stream of consciousness and a connection to the real you.

Experiencing that gap is one reason meditation is such a good thing to do. Quieting the mind and reflecting your self to your Self brings peace. Real peace. The kind of peace that doesn't make sense but cannot be denied.

When you are working in a "zone" and concentrating very hard on the task at hand (and only the task at hand), you are living in the moment, too. You may be using all of your faculties to accomplish the assignment, but you are not really there. You have temporarily merged with the activity, and in so doing opened yourself to inspiration that is flowing and helping you accomplish it. It is a wonderful feeling, and it's very productive. You wish you could do it all the time. If you are a creative, successful person, you make use of this ability a lot. You are tapping into your Higher Self, and it feels great. You can do this with lots of aspects of your life, and your life will be better for it.

I'm doing it as I write this book. Are you doing it as you read it? Are you fully embracing the message the words convey, or are you interrupting yourself to have a thought that's not connected?

You also step out of time when you become enthralled with a television program or are watching a movie. This is *not* a connection to your Higher Self, just the opposite. You may indeed be unaware of your surroundings and time certainly passes unnoticed, but this is because your brain has surrendered to input from the ego's world and this input is carefully designed to keep you asleep and control your thoughts for a period of time. The reader is highly encouraged to investigate the effect of television in particular on our ability to think critically. Needless to say, this will have a detrimental effect on our capacity to embrace our true reality.

Musing or daydreaming, on the other hand, is an excellent thing to do as long as it doesn't produce anxiety, worry or regret and it doesn't interfere with other things. It's another way to embrace the moment. Before we can accomplish our dreams, we have to dream them. Ideas that come from a place of inspiration lead us closer to our true nature as the author of our life.

Thoughts and actions that lead us away from our Higher Self feel bad in our heart. This doesn't mean that you don't have to do things that are distasteful if they are the right thing to do. Your heart of hearts will tell you the difference between something that is distasteful because it is wrong and something that may be unpleasant but is the right thing to do.

When we engage in activities that bring us closer to our true Self, they flow smoothly. We have a feeling that we are doing the right thing, we enjoy it, and it isn't stressful no matter how hard it is. Time seems to stop because we are living in the present moment and allowing communion with our Self. We can even take a break from time whenever we want just by focusing on the details of the moment.

What a wonderful natural ability we have. Could it be there for a reason?

> Fear is not of the present, but only of the past and future, which do not exist. There is no fear in the present when each instant stands clear and separated from the past, without its shadow reaching into the future. Each instant is a clean, untarnished birth, in which the Son of God emerges from the past into the present. And the present extends forever. It is so beautiful and so clean and free of guilt that nothing but happiness is there. No darkness is remembered, and immortality and joy are now.
>
> —*A Course in Miracles* T-15.2-8

Chapter 6

Reality

Nothing real can be threatened.
Nothing unreal exists.
Herein lies the peace of God.
—A Course in Miracles

Let's take a breather and recap. You know about your day-to-day reality with all its trials and pleasures and unconscious activities and hidden or obvious agendas. You also know that the temporary self who occupies this reality is not who you really are.

You have learned that you are not a body, you are not your thoughts, and you are not even your soul. You have learned that you are something hard to understand called the Decision Maker, and you have a little devil sitting on your shoulder called an ego.

You just learned that time doesn't exist except in the present moment, and you have learned how you naturally slip in and out of time every day. You now know that you can control this ability to some extent, and you can use it to improve your life experience here in the world.

You have also learned that basically everything you thought was real is not, but this hasn't helped you understand the nature of reality very well and it hasn't given you a new thought system to replace the one you just lost.

We have established that compared to your Awareness or your Greater Self, your ego-based, day-to-day reality is similar to a dream you have while sleeping. That's a great place to start our discussion of reality.

Try to imagine that you are really the Decision Maker and you are having a dream. This implies that you are asleep. In your sleep you have dreamed up a very real dream-world in which you are the central character. The entire universe and everything in it is part of your dream. It's a mega-dream. A really really big show. And it is very consistent. It goes on day after day. Same dream, different day.

Have you ever had the same dream night after night with each successive night pushing the plot just a little further? Can you remember how you felt when you woke up? Relief, right? "Oh, thank goodness it was just a dream; it seemed so real!" Then you forgot about it and got on with your day.

In reality, your life is a dream and your purpose is to wake up to the true nature of who you are.

So who are we? What is Awareness? Who is the Decision Maker?

Awareness is the "Christ Consciousness" in each of us. It is the place from which that feeling that we are more than what we perceive arises. It is that joyful suspicion that we just might be a lot more than what we perceive. Christ in this sense does not mean Jesus, although he could certainly be thought of as someone who embraced the Christ consciousness. In this sense we are all the Christ because at our essential core we are divine manifestations of the one life force.

We have all heard the phrase "the spirit of God is within you" but we don't know *where* it is inside us or how to access it very well. Whether you call it Awareness, the Presence, the Observer, your Heart of Hearts, your Higher Self or just your Self, it the same essential life force and you can feel it easily if not very strongly. In the Bible, Christ is referred to as the "Son of God." Your Awareness is your ego-veiled perception of your true heritage as a Son or Daughter of God as well.

The Decision Maker *is* the Christ, and again there is only one. This means that whether you are a man or woman, you are the Christ, the "Son" of God. So am I. So is everyone else. So is every*thing* else. The Child of God who decided to create an illusion that we call reality is still the one and only Child of the Source of All, even if it (reality) seems to be made up of millions of individual pieces. Our little life is not even the stuff of dreams compared to magnificence of God with whom His Child is one with Him. They are one single life force.

We are living a "dream of the separate self," but the immortal reality is that this "Child" and God have always been, and will always be, one. God's Creation *decided* to have an experience that we call life, but that doesn't mean that it stopped being God's Child, nor does it mean that God and His Child are actually separate. We could say that we are all one "in God," which is true, but that language presupposes the phrase "in this sense." This indicates that in another sense we are individuals, separate from God. That is not the lesson here. The lesson is that you *are* God. You are not separate in any way, period. This concept is called non-duality. In other words, there is God and nothing else. We forgot our heritage is all that happened. Our heritage did not forget us. Namasté literally means "I bow to you" and an actual bow is performed, in some cultures, as a sign of respect for the divinity that is in all of us.

Our ego is not a child of God. The ego is an illusion created by the real Child of God for a reason we'll explore later. It is the ego's subtle tricks that keep us from remembering our true heritage.

Non-duality means that you, me, that stone, the tree over there, the galaxy twinkling in the sky, the universe and every parallel universe we can imagine and everything we can't imagine are all *one* Son of God (to use Biblical language again).

This is a *big* thought, and it is a *big* change of perspective. It has big implications, too.

If there is only one, then by implication anything you do to another, you do to yourself, and vice versa. This one sounds familiar. Could it be the reason behind admonitions like "Love your neighbor as yourself" and "Do undo other as you would have them do unto you"? Could it also be the root cause of the concept of karma?

What if you really believed that you and your neighbor were equal children of God? What if you knew deep down that the only difference between you and the homeless person on the street was the nature of your temporary experience and that your permanent identities were identical? Can you understand how you and someone considered a monster like Hitler are the same? There is no essential difference, only temporal differences. Could this be what Jesus meant when he said, "A servant is not greater than his master; nor is he who is sent greater than he who sent him"?

You are everything and everything is you. This is the true meaning of Love.

What if we internalized this interpretation of reality and developed a personal identification of ourselves as Christ and taught that to our children? What if we taught them to recognize the Christ within and indoctrinated them with the firm belief that what they do to others they do to themselves because we are all one? What if they were able to look past the ego and see that everything in their Awareness *is* them and they loved it as themselves? What would that do to the human condition? For one thing, it might end conflict. It might feed the hungry. It might shelter the homeless and comfort the sick.

At this point in your understanding you can re-read some of the quotes from Jesus or Buddha or Mohammed or Krishna that seemed so hard to fathom in the past with your new understanding and get the message quite easily. Try it. It's fun.

If your true purpose is to "wake up" to who you really are, congratulate yourself! You have just taken a big first step. It's that simple. Your ego has told you it was difficult because waking up to your eternal reality spells the end of it. Now you know that "you" are the one who decides what happens, not the ego-you. You are the Dreamer, the Author, the Experiencer, the Awareness, the Decision Maker, and "you" are one with all that is; in fact, the real "you" is the one and only Child of God. That is enough to blow everything else out of your mind.

Now that you know this, everything will change, but your life will remain the same. You will still get up in the morning and make coffee. You will still go to school or work and engage in trivial or meaningful discourse. But something will be different.

You will feel better because the big picture has shifted. If you allow it, deep peace will come to you. Adversity won't seem so hard. Your faith that things will be okay will increase a thousand fold. You will feel no compunction to be right and little things won't bother you so much. You will know that everything that happens "outside" can only affect you "inside" if you let it. Your entire perspective can change if you want. In the same way that you can now understand Jesus' formerly cryptic messages, you can "see" the ego in operation in both yourself and other people if you try.

You do have to try. If this is your first time with these concepts, you have a lot of unwinding to do. You have spent a lifetime setting your unconscious beliefs firmly in place, and they won't go away because you had an epiphany. The ego is still with you. It isn't going anywhere either. It's going to lay low for a little while until the next "bad" thing happens so it can say: "Aha! I knew it! All that weird thinking was crazy, and you better forget about it and get back to your life!"

Trials in life are training for your little self to grow and embrace your higher Self in the same way that physical exercise is good for your body. You aren't going to get strong by sitting in a chair and thinking about it. You have to get up and work at it. Adversity is exercise for the little "you," and it provides the opportunity to retrain your mind. The harder the adversity the greater your progress can be.

You could also decide not to embrace these concepts and instead embrace your resistance to them. Life is a series of choices that came from a series of choices. You chose your reality every day, and if you chose to resist embracing your heritage, that is your option, too.

> There must be doubt before there can be conflict. And every doubt must be about yourself. Christ has no doubt, and from His certainty His quiet comes. He will exchange His certainty for all your doubts, if you agree that He is One with you, and that this Oneness is endless, timeless and within your grasp because your hands are His. He is within you, yet He walks beside you and before, leading the way that He must go to find Himself complete. His quietness becomes your certainty. And where is doubt when certainty has come?
>
> —*A Course in Miracles* T-24.V.9

The ancient Hindu story of Maya is instructive. It is a wonderful little fable that helps us understand how everything we have reviewed so far could possibly be so. It helps turn life into the game it should be. Until now we didn't know that we were playing a game. We didn't know the rules, and we didn't know how to succeed. Now we can begin to get the idea and learn to play.

Here is the story of Brahma and Maya as told by Don Miguel Ruiz in his book *The Mastery of Love*.

> There is an old story from India about the God, Brahma, who was all alone. Nothing existed but Brahma, and he was completely bored. Brahma decided to play a game, but there was no one to play the game with. So he created a beautiful goddess, Maya, just for the purpose of having fun, Once Maya existed and Brahma told her the purpose of her existence, she said, "Okay, let's play the most wonderful game, but you have to do what I tell you to do." Brahma agreed and following Maya's instructions, he created the whole universe. Brahma created the sun and the stars, the moon and the planets. Then he created life on earth: the animals, the oceans, the atmosphere, everything.
>
> Maya said, "How beautiful is this world of illusion you created. Now I want you to create a kind of animal that is so intelligent and aware that it can appreciate your creation." Finally Brahma created humans, and after he finished the creation, he asked Maya when the game was going to start.
>
> "We will start right now," she said. She took Brahma and cut him into thousands of teeny, tiny pieces. She put a piece inside every human and said, "Now the game begins! I am going to make you forget what you are, and you are

going to try to find yourself." Maya created the Dream, and still, even today, Brahma is trying to remember who he is. Brahma is there inside you, and Maya is stopping you from remembering what you are.

When you awake from the Dream, you become Brahma again, and reclaim your divinity. Then if Brahma inside you says, "Okay, I am awake; what about the rest of me?" you know the trick of Maya and you can share the truth with others who are going to wake up too.

Chapter 7

Resistance

> *What if you recognized that the world is an hallucination? What if you really understood you made it up? What if you realized that those who seem to walk about it in it, to sin and die, attack and murder and destroy themselves, are wholly unreal?*
>
> —*A Course in Miracles* T-13.I.3:2–7

We are resistant to our ultimate reality. We do not come easily to thoughts of oneness and egos, Higher Selves and Holy Spirits. We do not take seriously the idea that "life" is nothing more than a game being played by Brahma and Maya. The thought that you *are* God might even make you feel guilty for being so arrogant. The idea that life is an illusion similar to a dream we have when we sleep is ludicrous to the average person.

Everything we have learned in our life has supported the perception that just the opposite is true. We have believed what our eyes see, what our ears hear, and what we have been taught. We have all done this. How do we deny the evidence that the world exists? We can touch it and smell it and make an impression on it and on others. How could it not be real?

Some clarification may make these concepts a little easier to understand. First, we need to redefine the word "real" and the concept of "reality." Then we have to admit that we don't want to change the only reality we have ever known.

In the temporal sense the world is real. It is here, and you can touch it. But it is temporary. This planet, our solar system, the Milky Way galaxy, all galaxies and indeed the Universe itself will cease to exist at some point in time. In the very big picture, everything is temporary and in our day-to-day life everything is temporary, too. You are constantly changing, just like the world around you, and what is happening now will soon be different. Everything and everyone in our Universe is temporary—"real" for now but soon to evaporate into the mists of time and become "unreal." This is our common definition of reality. Reality as it exists in a temporal sense is always changing; therefore, it cannot be "real" except in the moment, and even then it is disappearing as fast as we perceive it.

Try to remember a time ten or fifteen or maybe even twenty years in the past. Think of an event that happened when you were a child or a significant birthday, or a baby being born. Imagine the situation and try to recall the color of the walls in the room or what the other people were wearing at the time. It is almost impossible to recall the details and it definitely isn't "real" anymore, except in your imagination. You can't touch it or affect it or measure it or smell it or see it, so it isn't "real" by any definition of the word.

If this is what happens to strong memories, what happens to your memories of your day-to-day life? They cannot be recalled at all. You probably can't even remember what you had for dinner last week, much less remember what you wore to work on the first Monday of September three years ago.

As we age, our vague recollections become a story that we tell ourselves and reminisce about with others. They are the subject of frequent revisions based on how we are feeling at the moment, and we aren't even aware that we are mentally rewriting our life story. We believe that is exactly how it was.

In the end we are left with an impression of the event based on prior recollections more than an actual memory of the event itself. These impressions are similar to a dream when compared to your memory of what happened to you just this morning. The only difference between the two is their distance in time from "right now."

Is it so hard to imagine that your whole life has more in common with a dream than with anything that we currently define as real?

If we define "real" to be eternal, then anything that isn't eternal isn't real, in any sense. This makes our day-to-day "reality" an illusion or a dream by comparison. The "now moment" itself may seem to be unreal and therefore illusory, because it too will soon join all previous now moments and fade into oblivion, becoming unreal. It is however replaced with yet another now moment in an endless series, making the now moment the *only* thing that is real here in the world because it alone has an eternal characteristic.

We know that everything is not as it seems to us. Just because we cannot see something or smell it or feel it, doesn't mean it isn't there. Ultra violet and gamma rays exist, but we can't perceive them without scientific instruments. We can easily admit that we don't know everything there is to know about the inner workings of our world much less our Universe, to say nothing of our immortal reality. Our immortal reality is that part of ourselves that isn't temporary, the part that is eternal.

When we speak of our Awareness of our consciousness and our decision, as the Decision Maker, to experience this temporary existence, we are looking at the decision from the perspective of our eternal Self, not our temporary day-to-day ego self. Our day-to-day self doesn't want to consider the temporary nature of our existence and compare it to eternity. That takes a lot of work! And it's impossible to know with any degree of certainty. This is what our ego tells us, and we listen.

Let's try to imagine "reality" in an eternal sense. "Eternal reality" would be a never-changing reality, and in order to grasp this idea our minds quickly collapse on one concept. The only concept we have of something eternal and unchanging is: God.

Omnipresent, omniscient, omnipotent, eternal, infinite, God. These are all concepts that we can't grasp. When we discuss our immortal reality, we are examining and trying to comprehend ideas we don't have the intellectual capacity to understand. We use words like "always," and "unlimited" and "forever" to soften the reality of the meaning, but they are the same impossible ideas. The concept of oneness with God and all that exists is another impossible idea, because it is directly related to immortality.

Our minds cannot grasp the concept of eternity. James Joyce does an impressive job of making this clear in his description of eternity from his book, *The Portrait of an Artist as a Young Man.*

> For ever! For all eternity! Not for a year or for an age but for ever. Try to imagine the awful meaning of this. You have often seen the sand on the seashore. How fine are its tiny grains! And how many of those tiny little grains go to make up the small handful which a child grasps in its play. Now imagine a mountain of that sand, a million miles high, reaching from the earth to the farthest heavens, and a million miles broad, extending to remotest space, and a million miles in thickness; and imagine such an enormous mass of countless particles of sand multiplied as often as there are leaves in the

> forest, drops of water in the mighty ocean, feathers on birds, scales on fish, hairs on animals, atoms in the vast expanse of the air: and imagine that at the end of every million years a little bird came to that mountain and carried away in its beak a tiny grain of that sand. How many millions upon millions of centuries would pass before that bird had carried away even a square foot of that mountain, how many eons upon eons of ages before it had carried away all? Yet at the end of that immense stretch of time not even one instant of eternity could be said to have ended. At the end of all those billions and trillions of years eternity would have scarcely begun. And if that mountain rose again after it had been all carried away, and if the bird came again and carried it all away again grain by grain, and if it so rose and sank as many times as there are stars in the sky, atoms in the air, drops of water in the sea, leaves on the trees, feathers upon birds, scales upon fish, hairs upon animals, at the end of all those innumerable risings and sinkings of that immeasurably vast mountain not one single instant of eternity could be said to have ended; even then, at the end of such a period, after that eon of time the mere thought of which makes our very brain reel dizzily, eternity would scarcely have begun.

In this incomparably graphic description of eternity, we can see how woefully inadequate is our ability to conceptualize ideas that approach infinity. We can understand on an academic level and we even have math that uses concepts that our minds cannot truly grasp.

Far from being a romantic excursion into the boundless bliss of God, Joyce's description lays bare the potential for eternity to be a brutal kind of boredom harkening from the depths of hell. Whether we love the idea of eternity or are scared to death of it, this description serves to impress upon us the degree of our intellectual incompetence on the subject. Just because we cannot conceive of eternity doesn't mean it doesn't exist; and no one is claiming that eternity isn't "real" in every sense of the term.

The problem we have is finding a secure place for ourselves in this concept. We can't even imagine it, so projecting ourselves into it is equally impossible. This creates real, solid, and mostly unconscious resistance to all concepts that attempt to do so.

Biblical descriptions of heaven and eternity are glossed over by the average believer and accepted with lip service to faith. But when pressed, most would admit that an eternity in heaven, even if it is at the right hand of God Almighty, is not a pleasant prospect. The ego stops here. Resistance is complete. The answers are unknown and unknowable.

The ego, that little devil on your shoulder, has no place in eternity. His place is in the temporary world. The ego *is* our belief that the world is real. "You" have a place in eternity, even if you cannot conceive of what it is, because "you" are not your ego. Your ego doesn't want you to know this. Its counsel is to forget about eternity and focus on the world. It is easy advice to take. All we have to do is believe that real satisfaction can be found here in the world of form. Then we can search but not find it, for "eternity."

The simple fact is that eternity exists and so do we, but neither of these concepts are as we imagine them with our limited capacity. It is only the ego that feeds our need to understand them. The ego is using the unknowable as a deflection to keep us from realizing that we don't have to be able to comprehend eternity to embrace our place in it.

It is our collective ego that makes eternity sound interminable to a hellish extent. In the same way that a mosquito cannot comprehend the theory of relativity, we cannot imagine our true heritage. This doesn't make it untrue or unreal in the eternal sense. True eternal reality is not concerned with anything temporary. Only our ego is concerned with things that are temporary.

Compared to a reality that is eternal, our little existence here and now is an illusion. If we expand our thinking and just touch the concept of eternity, we will know with certainty that everything really is just one. We are resistant, but that resistance is thinner than you think. It can be passed through. The only thing that is infinite, eternal, and immortal is God. If it exists, it is God. If it isn't God, it doesn't exist. This is non-duality. Pure, simple, perfect.

Our inability to "understand" eternity is a blessing. Our physical brain cannot understand eternity, infinity, immortality, oneness, and God, but this doesn't mean that we can't. Dwelling (with our day-to-day mind) on an incomprehensible idea like eternity is actually the key to a door. The door leads to higher awareness and perceptions that cannot be understood by the brain. They can be understood by "you," just not in the same way you understand things in the world. It is a different kind of perception, that's all. It comes into your world as deep peace. It manifests as a feeling of expansion of the spirit. These comparisons are weak and do not do the concept justice. Our perception of our immortality is indefinable because there is nothing here that compares to it.

Anything that brings you near that door, much less gives you a key to open it, is terrifying to your ego. The ego made the temporary world, and that's all it understands. Eternity cannot be conceived by the ego and therefore it isn't real to it. Anything that threatens its world, like you embracing eternity, is met with resistance. Thoughts of how impossible eternity is to understand, and the valueless nature of trying, are resistant thoughts coming from your ego. They are very effective. All egos feel this way and they may band together to "talk you out if it." When you listen to a friend instead of your Self and go against your intuitive (Higher Self) feelings, you are surrendering to your resistance that you are greater than you perceive and admitting that you are no greater than your ego.

The concept of eternity becomes a key that unlocks the door to higher awareness precisely because it cannot be understood by the ego. "You" have Higher Self and ego thoughts. You listen to the ego thoughts because they are very loud and they come in concepts that relate to the world. Higher Self thoughts do not come to our awareness in this way. They are subtle, and you feel them more than think them. Intuition is a form of Higher Self "thought," but it isn't a thought. It is more a feeling that you cannot justify.

When you dwell on the concept of infinity or God, you feel your way into it and embrace those feelings while removing any "thoughts" that may accompany them. This gives the ego no room to maneuver and puts it on the sidelines temporarily. With the ego out of the way, those higher perceptions can manifest in our being.

One way to do this is to ask questions that have no answer and pursue them, with your brain, to the natural conclusion that these concepts are unknowable. Use these kinds of thoughts to lead your ego away and then sit back to experience the sensations that remain.

Who am "I"? (I don't know.) Who is this "I" that thinks it is a person in the world? (I don't know.) Where did it come from? (I don't know.) If this "I" is consciousness, what is consciousness? (I don't know.) What is Awareness? (Awareness is my feeling that I am greater than I perceive.) Who is having this Awareness feeling? (I don't know.) Who is this greater self that feels this? (I don't know.) Where did it come from? (It came from God.) What is God? (I don't know.)

The ego doesn't know! "You" can begin to "know" when you stop trying to define it and surrender to the feeling that you don't know, but that's okay. It can't be known, and that's okay, too. It feels good. It feels timeless. It feels peaceful. It feels right. Embrace those feelings and quiet down the thoughts. Just experience the unknowable, immortal being-ness that is "you" with no words or thoughts and no ego. This is the key.

Our ultimate job in the world is to, in the words of *A Course in Miracles*, "deny the denial of truth." In other words, stop resisting! Stop giving "head-room" to resistant thoughts. Allow your imagination to expand. Allow your Awareness of your immortality to lead you to the *feeling* that "you" are the Decision Maker who chose to live apart from God. Allow yourself to feel, just for a second, that you are God's only Child and you are *not* separate from Him, and see what happens.

You don't have to stop living life as we know it to do this. You do have to expand your thinking just a little bit and resist that resistance just by noticing it. True peace only comes from the eternal, and you don't have to understand it to enjoy it. If you allow it, the same eternity from which everything comes can come to you and bring with it real joy and peace and love.

Our ego is scared to death of eternity, and that makes us afraid of it, too. Everyone is naturally afraid of the unknown. We try and try to make our world clean and organized so that we can control it and understand it, or we get comfortable with the disorganization and we love that. We don't want to exchange the only reality we have ever known for something unknown, especially if it is incomprehensible and the part that has been explained to us sounds like a fate worse than death.

We are resistant to deep spiritual truth not because we cannot understand it, although that gives us a ready excuse. We are resistant because the ego (our resistance to eternal reality) is interfering with our ability to understand with our temporary mind. The ego is the loudest, most insistent part of our day-to-day mind, and it does *not* want "you" to approach these ideas at all.

This will manifest in most spiritual seekers' study of any path that leads out of the dream of the separate self. Resistance takes many forms. Procrastination is one. We just can't seem to find time to study. When we do we have trouble concentrating and are easily distracted. We may have to reread the same paragraph multiple times or ask the teacher to repeat themselves. Our resistance causes us to misremember critical ideas and we subconsciously change the meaning to one that is in alignment with our ego's desire to make the dream real. We try to use the message to create "heaven on earth." We don't want to believe that there is no earth except in our imagination.

Sometimes we will not be able to understand a concept at all. We just don't "get it" so we decide we're not smart enough to learn and may abandon the effort. In rare cases fear in the form of a noticeable anxiety may set in when we read or talk about certain ideas. Continuous searching for truth by reading yet another book or attending another seminar may be resistance at work. As far as the ego is concerned it is okay to seek but it is not okay to find.

By far the most common form of resistance is an inability to remember the concepts the lessons are teaching. In other words we have trouble remembering what we have just learned. People with wonderful brains and strong memories for all kinds of difficult concepts (as they pertain to the world) will notice that they are unable to keep even the simplest of ideas pertaining our actual eternal reality in mind for long and they are forgotten almost instantly. This is one reason I wrote *Heart of Hearts*. I realized that my resistance was too strong to overcome by simply studying. I needed a way to cement the ideas in my conscious mind.

Forgetfulness is probably happening to you as you read this book and understand the concepts. They just do not want to stick! You may be able to recall names and dates and even mathematical formulas with ease, but for some reason you cannot explain or clearly remember what your ego or your Awareness is, even though the past four chapters have explained it in numerous ways. The upcoming concepts of forgiveness and atonement will be even more slippery.

Part of this is the fact that the lessons are new and the topic is unfamiliar, but you integrate new information every day. The real reason is that your ego has a very strong resistance, and that means you do, too. This resistance derails all but the most devoted seekers, and it can take lifetimes of study to get past it. Dedication is the key. Practice is the only thing that is needed. Your ego is not all-powerful. "You" are all-powerful, and if you really want to understand your immortal reality you can do it. It isn't as hard as many things in life, and it will get easier as you work on it. Soon you will see and feel your ego's resistance start to melt.

You don't have to fight your ego and try to win a struggle for the salvation of your immortal soul to accomplish this. Indeed, actively resisting your ego makes it even more real and powerful, and you will not succeed. Noticing when we are being led by our ego is all we need to do. If we can just see when we are thinking or acting under the direction of the ego, we give ourselves the opportunity to chose a different teacher; in other words, a different way of thinking. That's all. We'll discuss this more in the chapter on Special Relationships and Overcoming the Ego.

How can we open up to our immortal reality and allow it to improve our life? First we have to learn about the concepts of Separation, Forgiveness and Atonement. These ideas require that you do nothing except change your mind about the nature of "reality" and accept that we all have a resistance to truth.

> What makes this world seem real except your own denial of the truth that lies beyond? What but your thoughts of misery and death obscure the perfect happiness and the eternal life your Father wills for you? And what could hide what cannot be concealed except illusion? What could keep from you what you already have except your choice to see it not, denying it is there?
>
> The Thought of God created you. It left you not, nor have you ever been apart from it an instant. It belongs to you. By it you live. It is your Source of life, holding you one with it and everything is one with you because it left you not. The Thought of God protects you, cares for you, makes soft your resting place and smooth your way, lighting your mind with happiness and love. Eternity and everlasting life shine in your mind, because the Thought of God has left you not, and still abides with you.
>
> —*A Course in Miracles* W-165.1.1–4;2.1–7

Chapter 8

Separation

> *The thoughts you think are in your mind, as you are in the mind that thought of you. And so there are no separate parts in what exists within God's Mind. It is forever One, eternally united and at peace.*
>
> —*A Course in Miracles* T-30.III6 7–9

Merriam-Webster's Dictionary defines *separation* as, "the state of being separated," which it further defines as "to set or keep apart." That is what has happened to "you." You have been *separated* from your Source and you are being "kept apart" from it.

You believe you are a *separate* individual. Everything around you supports this conclusion. You appear to live in a bubble in your head and no one else can enter. You can get to know someone, but you cannot become them. As a society, we celebrate our individuality. We teach it to our children and encourage everyone to believe that they are separate individuals walking a unique path. We value one-of-a-kind objects or performances or experiences.

We do not seem to value "sameness." We seem to actively work to avoid it. A woman who finds that she is wearing the same dress as another woman at a party might actually leave. There are so many options when buying a car that almost none are exactly the same. Everyone wears a different style of shoe, and eyeglasses reflect the unique personality of their owners. In reality we only allow differences to appear within the tight boundaries of conformity to our social norms. Those who are perceived as significantly different, like homeless people or those with mental illness, are shunned.

These attitudes work day and night to ensure that we feel unique, special, and separate from every other human being, while at the same time fostering a feeling of community with those who are similar to us. They are reinforced at every turn in the dream world, yet we just established that we are *not* separate from anyone else; in fact, we are one!

So why would our entire society be oriented to communicate the exact opposite message? Is there any "thing" that might suffer if "you" understood that "you" are not separate from anyone or anything?

Separation from God is the real problem. This is the one the ego doesn't want you to see. Making sure that all the "evidence" in the outer world points away from oneness is just a smokescreen. It keeps you busy and far away from the idea that the real crisis is that we seem to be separate from our Source and we will never be whole until we reunite.

The reason the peace and joy and love you do experience in the outer world are fleeting glimpses of the real thing is you are trying to find "true satisfaction" in a life that is little more than a dream compared to your "real" world. We are the one Child of God but forgot who we are (for a reason we'll explore in a minute), and we think we are separate individuals. How could the Christ, even if she forgot her heritage, possibly be satisfied with anything less than total reunification with God the Father? She can't. And you can't, and neither can I; that's why nothing in the world can truly satisfy us.

Separation is the root cause of everything. The "tiny mad idea" that we can exist as separate from God gave rise to the ego in the first place. That gave rise to the universe of form, which in turn gave rise to us.

Our mission, should we choose to accept it, is to go back in our mind to that instant when we chose to be a separate individual and change our mind and decide not to be separate anymore. It is not against the rules to change your mind. In fact, it is your greatest purpose. If you want to realize your immortal reality as the one Child of God, then you have to stop dreaming that you are a separate individual and wake up to your inheritance by changing your mind and making the decision for God and *not* for the ego this time.

How? You must "forgive" everything. Before we discuss how true forgiveness works, let's pause for a moment to explore how we got in this predicament in the first place. I'll use the masculine gender (Biblical style) for the sake of simplicity, but feel free to substitute the feminine in your mind as you read, if you would like. These concepts are, of course, gender neutral.

How did the Son of God become separated from his Creator?

The answer is that he didn't separate, and he isn't separate now. God and His Son are one Supreme Being. They always were and still are. When you understand in your heart of hearts that "you" aren't separate from your creator either, you have reached "atonement," which is the goal of our life.

The only difference between Christ and God the Father is that the Son did not create the Father. Besides that they are identical. This concept is called non-duality, meaning "not more than one," and we've mentioned it before. It is confusing, right?

Okay, here's what happened. One day the Son was having a wonderful time being the Son of God, when he had a thought.

This thought was different than his usual Son-of-God thoughts. This thought was a little crazy. He actually stopped to consider if he could separate from the Father and live alone, as it were. Then he said: “Ummm. No thanks.” And he went back to being blissful.

But that tiny, “insane” idea that maybe he could be separate was born in that instant because it was thought by the Son of God. If he thinks it, then suddenly we have Big Bangs and Universes and Time and Class M Planets and Sentient Life Forms and Pain and Triumph and Life and Death and Love and Hate and Good and Bad and Summer and Winter and Happiness and Sadness and the whole big dualistic world we know and love! But only for a split second, as he considered the idea. Then it went away. “We” are in a “dream” about that split second.

This is an overly simplistic version, but it helps us understand some very complex thoughts. We “get” how the Decision Maker/ Dreamer is the Son who never separated from the Father in the first place. It explains why he, i.e. “you,” can’t be truly fulfilled by anything in the world of form (because it doesn’t exist). And it shows us where we’re going because we are already there. “We” never left. In our dream mind, we’re still in that split second, and that’s why we think we are here.

The ego appeared then, too, and it has been trying to convince us that the world is not a dream, that we are actually here, and this is as good as it gets, from the very beginning. The ego goes away as soon as we truly understand that “we” made it all up, so it has been working feverishly to make sure we don’t figure that out.

The ego uses guilt and hate and fear to make sure we stay asleep. For this reason the ego is sometimes referred to as the “parasite.” The Universe actually appeared, during that split second, because the ego suggested to the Son that he better hide from the Father who, the ego said, was going to be very angry that he had that thought of separating. The Son, believing him, created the universe and went there to hide.

The physical world the Son created was formed under the direction of the ego. Because of this, it is filled with strife and guilt and sickness and pain and grief and loss and brief moments of false hope. This keeps our attention diverted from who we really are, as the Decision Making Son of God, and convinces us that we are weak, insignificant sinners who should thank our lucky stars to even be alive and not ever hope for anything more. This insane belief is what the ego has managed to achieve for most of recorded history.

Very few have ever transcended the ego and realized who they truly are. The theological giants like Buddha and Jesus have achieved enlightenment along with less well-known modern individuals like Eckhart Tolle and Adyashante, and poets like Wordsworth and Shakespeare, but the vast majority remains sound asleep with no idea of their birthright. The ego set this up so well that it is almost impossible to wake up. Almost, but not quite.

Chapter 9

Holy Spirit

> *The happy dreams the Holy Spirit brings are different from the dreaming of the world, where one can merely dream he is awake.*
>
> —*A Course in Miracles* W140.3:1

When the "Son" had that small little thought that he could separate and the ego appeared and began whispering, God created the memory of who we are and tossed it into the mix. That memory is called the Holy Spirit. "His" sole purpose is to help you remember that you are the one and only Child of God, that you never left the Father, and that you are only dreaming this whole thing. You can wake up any time you want. Or you can stay asleep and dream this dream for as long as you want. It is completely up to you.

When you are ready to wake up, the Holy Spirit will be there to help. The Holy Spirit is a symbol, of course. "She" is the memory of our true heritage as the Christ within everyone. The ego is a symbol, too. It is our resistance to truth. Neither the Holy Spirit nor the ego are real in the true sense of the word, but they are helpful devices that we can use to understand why we are here and how to get home.

The Holy Spirit is not a feeling we are conscious of, like the sensitivity one might have of one's Awareness of being. Rather the Holy Spirit's (very real) existence is confirmed in the changes to our world that result from following its teachings and asking for its help.

The true ontological reality is that there is only One and that is God. Anything else is not real. That doesn't help us very much here on Plato's playground, however, so we are going to use the Holy Spirit concept as if she were a real person who has a secret system that we can use to get back where we started.

> God gave his teacher to replace the one you made, not to conflict with it. And what he would replace has been replaced. Time lasted but an instant in your mind, with no effect upon eternity. And so is all time past, and everything exactly as it was before the way to nothingness was made. The tiny tick of time in which the first mistake was made, and all of them within that one mistake, held also the Correction for that one, and all of them that came within the first. And in that tiny instant time was gone, that was all it ever was. What God gave answer to is answered and is gone.
>
> —*A Course in Miracles* T-26.V.3

That secret system the Holy Spirit has is a little technique called *forgiveness*.

Chapter 10

Forgiveness

> *Seek not to change the world, but choose to change your mind about the world.*
>
> —*A Course In Miracles* T21.in.1:7

The Holy Spirit's forgiveness is different than yours.

Your forgiveness pardons a perceived slight. Someone steps on your toe by accident and, noticing what they have done, says, "I'm so sorry! Please excuse me." You say, "No problem," and let them off the hook.

Maybe something bigger than an accidental toe crunch happens, and the other person doesn't apologize. You are then advised to "take the high road" and forgive them their sin of being inconsiderate.

Worldly forgiveness lets other people off the hook even though they were wrong.

This concept has been held up by society as the one true way to achieve grace. We forgive in order to be forgiven.

> And (let us off the hook for) our trespasses as we (let others off the hook) who have trespassed against us.

The reward for forgiving in this manner (besides eternal bliss in heaven) is that the person doing the forgiving can at least try to feel like the bigger person.

That's hard if someone maliciously hurt you or someone in your family, stole something from you, stabbed you in the back at work, or harmed your child. You might even consider these and other lesser crimes "unforgivable" even if the person apologizes. In fact, you hope they won't, because then you won't feel so guilty "getting even" with them.

Wars have been fought for less than the crimes mentioned above. Family and tribal feuds can go on for generations. In our "civilized society," we can take our grievances to court and agree to abide by the decision. The court can assign blame and mandate compensation, but they cannot make the feeling of offence go away. Only you can make the feeling of offence go away.

If someone screws up in a minor way, and they own up to it and say they are sorry, your feeling of offence will clear quickly. If you screw up, admit it, beg someone's pardon and receive it, you might feel guilty for a little while but it will lift and all will be fine.

We tend to be much better at forgiving than we are at asking for forgiveness. If someone accepts responsibility, apologizes, and begs forgiveness, we are usually willing to grant it quickly because we know how awful it feels to be on that side of the interaction.

If we are the person who must ask for forgiveness, we will search our soul for a way to avoid it. We just hate to admit we are wrong and to ask for pardon, and our ego will do a lot to avoid it. When we do it, we are usually caught dead to rights and have no other option than a big mea culpa that we usually couch with our excuse. "I shouldn't have said that—but I was drunk."

Sometimes a person will do something and apologize if they get caught to avoid or reduce the punishment. This kind of apology is sometimes so heartfelt and sincere we question its authenticity.

We have lots of examples of public figures getting caught with their pants down (sometimes literally) who realize that the fastest way to make the problem go away is to accept responsibility and beg forgiveness without any excuse. Now we have to decide whether to let the person off the hook or not. It doesn't matter if "we" are the public, the court system, the spouse or the children of the offender; the decision is the same.

Except for a sincere acceptance of responsibility and a true and humble apology that results in a kind of forgiveness that makes the problem vanish as if it never happened, the whole idea of this kind of forgiveness doesn't work.

We don't like to admit that we are wrong, whether it is to our friends, our family, our partner, or our boss, because when someone forgives us we feel smaller than them. If we have judged them to have lower status than us, this feeling is repulsive. If we have judged them to have equal or higher status, the feeling is regretful. Either way it is unpleasant. In *A Course in Miracles* the kind of forgiveness we have been discussing is called forgiveness-to-destroy.

Forgiveness-to-destroy is a top-down problem with God at the beginning. We are told He will forgive our "sins" if we ask. We are told that unlike people, God forgives us no matter what we did or how badly we apologize and accept responsibility. God is so "big" about that. He makes us feel so small and guilty. To top it off, we don't ever have any direct impression of His forgiveness aside from the fleeting feeling of relief for having asked. In the back of our mind, we wonder if He really forgave us, and we suspect that He is kind of like us and doesn't truly forgive at all. Maybe He holds grudges just like we do!

Forgiveness-to-destroy in all its myriad manifestations is unsatisfying to our heart of hearts and is a spawn of the ego, not your Higher Self or the Holy Spirit.

True forgiveness releases the other person and yourself from the purgatory of sin, guilt and fear. The world's definition of forgiveness doesn't accomplish this very well, so let's look at a different way of thinking about it and see if we can accomplish that objective.

Chapter 11

Real Forgiveness

> *It is your forgiveness that will bring the world of darkness to the light. It is your forgiveness that lets you recognize the light in which you see. Forgiveness is the demonstration that you are the light of the world. Through your forgiveness does the truth about yourself return to your memory. Therefore, in your forgiveness lies your salvation.*
>
> —*A Course in Miracles* W-62.1.1–5

True forgiveness has nothing to do with letting people off the hook. You should still let people off the hook and never hold grudges, and you can still beg for pardon but don't expect that it will deliver any kind of lasting peace. Don't believe that it makes you a greater person to forgive in this way or a lesser one if you must ask for another's forgiveness.

Remember, we are all one consciousness experiencing our temporary existence in different forms in what amounts to a dream compared to our true reality as the Christ.

The reason you cannot let someone off the hook except the way the ego tells you is because there is no hook! The "outside" condition is a story that you are authoring. It isn't "real." The "real" you is just watching the movie, dreaming the dream, experiencing the experience. How do you take offence and forgive something that happened in a movie or a novel or a dream? You don't. You experience it, and you let it go.

Maybe a movie makes you feel angry or sad or jealous or happy or victorious, but you don't consider it "real." You go to the movies and read books because you want to have a "pretend" emotional experience that is outside of "reality" so you can enjoy it. It wouldn't be any fun and you wouldn't go to the movie if that didn't happen.

Life is like that. "You" as the Dreamer are making up an exciting story called *Your Life* and watching as it unfolds and the characters experience the emotions associated with the story. The real "you" doesn't have any vested interest in who wins or loses or succeeds or perishes, because it knows that it is only so much cosmic celluloid.

Who weeps when their character dies or feels true remorse for their actions in the MMORPG of the moment? There is no question that one can experience intense excitement and a heightened emotional response while playing today's computer games. However, unless they have unknowingly substituted their personality for an artificial creation in the game world, players leave their game persona in the game when they are finished playing.

True forgiveness is recognizing that what we call "reality" is an illusion in the same way that an online game is a fantasy, not real life. Forgiveness is understanding that we created the entire script and cast of characters and that we are not actually separate from anyone or anything, especially God. When we truly grasp this concept and internalize it, we see our enemies and our idols and everything in between as ourselves in a creation of our own minds.

> The mind without the body cannot make mistakes. It cannot think that it will die, nor be the prey of merciless attack. Anger becomes impossible, and where is terror then? What fears could still assail those who have lost the source of all attack, the core of anguish and

> the seat of fear? Only forgiveness can relieve the mind of thinking that the body is its home. Only forgiveness can restore the peace that God intended for His holy Son. Only forgiveness can persuade the Son to look again upon his holiness.
>
> —*A Course in Miracles* W-pI.192.5:1-7

This process of forgiveness is not a part of our society's consciousness, and we have trouble internalizing the reality of it. Just in this book, we have been through the logic of life being a dream in a number of different ways. While we were doing that, you understood and it made sense and felt good. Now it's kind of fuzzy, and you are having trouble buying into it—again.

This is normal. It is resistance at work. Your ego is interfering again. Your ego *is* part of your day-to-day consciousness. It is ninety percent or more of a person's consciousness. It is also deeply imbedded in your subconscious. This means that your ego, *your resistance to truth*, has infiltrated your core thinking and feeling structures.

For this reason, forgiveness is also a process of mind training where we learn to let go; in other words, surrender our egoic need to control and judge and fear. It requires practice. We have spent a lifetime listening to the ego tell us the dream is true. We have learned to believe that what our eyes see and what our thoughts think are real.

Luckily, the Holy Spirit (as the memory of our true reality) is inside us to remind us of our identity as the Christ and lead us back to the place we never left. (Does it make sense this time around?) This all happens in our mind. It is an internal process that has been compared to peeling layers off of an onion. There is nothing that we need "do" in the outside world of form. Forgiveness happens inside our mind or not at all. Healing happens internally, and we gradually become peaceful, humble, and grateful inside. Our brow un-furrows and in our joy, we project warmth and love.

We must still handle what the ego-world throws our way. For a while, it might be quite severe as our ego has a "storm" and everything seems to go wrong in our life. This is actually very common. It is an early test of our commitment to awaken from the "dream of the separate self."

The Holy Spirit uses the world as a classroom where we learn our forgiveness lessons and where we use adversity to move forward. Any kind of painful challenge in life is an opportunity to practice forgiveness. This means that we tell ourselves that whatever problem or unpleasant feeling we are having is not "real," and, whether it is caused by us or not, it is only a device to make us *think* the dream is true. Then we ask the Holy Spirit to help us accept this concept as true and let go of the negative feeling. We ask for help to release our ego. We wait for that to happen. It will. The Holy Spirit's presence gets stronger as we call on it more often, and that's good because the ego tests never stop.

Adversity, hardship, sickness, misfortune, jealousy, anger, envy, blame, scorn, judgment, fear, resentment, anxiety, mistrust, despair, apathy, pride, aggression and the like are all "ego traps." Anytime we find ourselves thinking that the story is real, we have fallen into one of the many traps our ego has set for us and it is, yet again, time to forgive.

> I must have decided wrongly because I am not at peace. I made this decision myself but I can also decide otherwise because I want to be at peace. I do not feel guilty, because the Holy Spirit will undo all the consequences of my wrong decision if I will let him. I choose to let him by allowing him to decide for God for me.
>
> —*A Course in Miracles* T.5.VII.6:7-11

It is not a matter of what the world or the ego throws at us. All kinds of trials and tribulations are going to come our way, along with plenty of opportunities and beautiful sunny days. What is important is how we react to them *inside*. Are you upset? Do you feel persecuted? Do you lash out? If so, the ego has won because you are admitting that the dream is real and reacting to it.

On the other hand we could see these adversities for what they are, a test of the courage of our convictions. If we bring our anxieties and doubts to the Holy Spirit and ask for help to release them, if we realize that the crises we experience are actually happening in our mind (and only in our mind), and if we remind ourselves of who we are on a regular basis, then we will begin to feel the peace the Holy Spirit brings. This is genuine internally generated peace. It is not dependant on positive external conditions but is forged strong as steel in the fire of negative situations.

As far as the world is concerned, you may appear to be happier as you learn to recognize the ego's knee-jerk reaction to every situation and let it storm through without responding. The ego is actually easy to see because it always reacts the strongest to any situation. The ego's reaction comes a split second *after* your heart of hearts. You *knew* the right answer immediately, but it was overwhelmed by the ego's reaction and you lost track of it. It vanished in the ego's tornado. If you wait and calm down and look within, you can also recognize the Holy Spirit's response because your heart of hearts agrees with it.

Remember, there are no "right" or "wrong" decisions, only ego or Higher Self decisions. Ego decisions are known as "wrong-minded," and decisions made with the help of the Holy Spirit are known as "right-minded." Decisions that seem to spring from the ego can still be right-minded if they have the effect of moving you closer to your true reality as the Christ. You are in a classroom because you are learning. You still think there are answers to questions. You have not realized that all "answers" eventually become "right" because they always lead you to realize who you are. Some answers simply move you along faster and with less difficulty than others.

To make a decision with your heart of hearts, you cannot rely on logic. You must think about it with your rational mind to be sure, but "you" already know; you just aren't in touch with it. Try calming your mind and removing judgment. In other words, forgive the decision. That means let it go and remember that this is an opportunity to practice forgiveness by realizing that you are not separate from anyone or anything, especially God. Then, and this is the most important step, ask the Holy Spirit (or Jesus or your Higher Self or your Heart of Hearts) for help do the thing that will reinforce this concept in your life. In other words pray for guidance to do the thing that will bring you closer to your true Self. It is the only prayer that God can grant, and it will result in the best outcome for all concerned.

The answer was the quiet knowing that came in the fraction of a second before the ego jumped in and grabbed your attention. Go back to that! That was your Higher Self knowing immediately what to do. Follow it. It is never wrong. And it won't let you starve. Fear lets you starve. Your Higher Self takes care of you.

Although you may be able to justify a Higher Self decision, it is not made logically. It is not carefully considered in the traditional sense. You must admit, however, that many of your "regrets" in life stem from not listening to your inner guide. You did what others or your pride (ego) thought was right and convinced yourself.

Let yourself off the hook for your regrets. Forgive your guilt. You learned from it and that is good. Realize that the so called "bad" decision resulted in a greater understanding of your higher purpose and rejoice in it. Then let it go.

Always follow the path of least *internal* resistance. This is the path toward God, and even if it is the more difficult choice in the temporal world, it will seem easier and things will fall into place almost of their own accord.

You will know that you are making a right-minded decision when a peaceful feeling follows, even if it is expensive, seems wrong, and is fraught with difficulty. You will have doubts, but you know it is right. You know that you will have the strength when you need it and you do it with a clear conscious. This is real faith, and you can't miss it when it arrives. When you trust in that faith, you have "trust-in-faith."

Trust-in-Faith

Trust-in-faith is a root-cause concept. It is a core belief. It is one of a precious few foundations upon which all effects in your life spring. Trust-in-faith reaches much further than just doing the right thing. It knows that everything that happens is good. Even if it feels bad, seems wrong, and inadvertently goes against Higher Self knowing, trust-in-faith understands that there is a lesson involved. Our job is to learn the lesson, not behave perfectly in every situation. The lesson will result in spiritual growth, and spiritual growth is always good.

We do not know for certain why things happen in our life. Life is very unpredictable and we get caught unprepared all the time. Sometimes something "good" happens, like a rainy day that unexpectedly blows over when we arrive at our destination, or we get bumped up to first class on the airplane. Other times something "bad" happens, like someone crashes into our car, the furnace goes out, or we get reprimanded at work.

When you have *faith* that things always happen for a good reason, even if you don't understand it at the time, and you *trust* that the effect will be beneficial and lead to spiritual growth, then you have embraced trust-in-faith. It isn't necessary to ultimately understand the reason, although sometimes it seems to become apparent as time goes by. Many people have had the experience of losing a job and being devastated by the loss, only to find an even better job. Maybe that new job leads one to find a mate. Now the "devastating" job loss seems like a wonderful thing.

Trust-in-faith applies that "knowing" (that everything is going to turn out just fine) to everything "bad" that happens, immediately after it occurs, no matter what it is. It places trust in the fact that right-minded thinking will bring lessons that must be learned. Those lessons might feel bad, but they will always result in a greater good for all concerned. This deep faith clears our minds and allows us to release the belief that is causing the lesson in the first place. The deeper our faith in this reality, the easier it is to trust that the "bad" thing happened for a good reason. Trust-in-faith puts your future in the hands of God and relaxes in the certainty that all will be well.

It is very hard sometimes to tell the difference between ego and Higher Self intuitions. We do the best we can, but we misjudge all the time. Trust-in-faith allows you to understand that the reason that you made a mistake and caused something negative to enter your life is because you are teaching yourself a lesson. Lessons can be learned, and that relieves the need for them to recur. This makes even the most terrible lesson "good" in the sense that it is an opportunity for forward progress.

Trust-in-faith is a core-foundation, root-cause belief. If you have it, it will carry you through the "worst" of times with relative ease. It will allow you to release anxiety and fear (if they arise at all) by simply embracing your trust in faith. There is no cause below trust-in-faith driving it, as if it were an effect. Effects may seem to drive other effects, but when one looks deeply, there is always a cause that is driving them. Many times it is a lack of trust-in-faith. In other words, if we do not have it, it drives negative effects. Certain conditions, like your religious convictions, may allow you to embrace the concept of trust-in-faith, but those convictions do not cause it. It is a cause in itself. Causes drive effects.

Fear is an effect of the lack of trust-in-faith. Anxiety is an effect of fear. Anxiety drives negative thoughts and behaviors, which result in "bad" things happening. The "bad" effects may cause regret or guilt, which are also effects. This may lead you to project the responsibility ("It's all your fault!") as the ego pulls out its best trick for making you feel better: blame, which is, of course, another effect. The lack of trust-in-faith is the root cause of all of these effects.

These effects are actually pointing to the lesson that there is a lack of trust-in-faith that exists as a core belief. Changing this core belief, in other words, changing the *cause* of the effects, will relieve the necessity for them. Changing that belief, even a little bit, will have a positive effect. Changing that belief a lot, and embracing it as a certainty, will turn the lessons positive. In this case, your inner attitude becomes peace filled and joyful, and "good" things happen.

Trust in faith leads to gratitude. You are grateful that you recognize trying situations as opportunities in the first place. You are thankful for the lesson they give you the chance to learn. You might not get the lesson but that does not diminish the appreciation for having been offered the opening. Gratitude for all things is trust in faith embodied.

A number of years ago I found myself living alone for the first time in my life, and I was in my forties! Since it wasn't my idea, it was a shock, and my ego reacted with every usual trap. I was lonely. I was scared. I was angry. I felt victimized. I was anxious and uncertain. I tried to cope in a rational way, but the truth was that I took very little responsibility and blamed my problems on everyone else. I tried desperately to hang onto everything I thought I had lost. Things were not going well. These obvious projections were not making me feel better ,and in fact, additional events started happening to make me feel worse. My money ran out, and my obligations grew. I was in a state of almost constant stress. I sought solace in alcohol and "fun times." I escaped into work and romantic interludes in an attempt to rebuild my self-confidence. None of it worked.

I began meditating, and I learned how to forgive. I let myself off the hook in the traditional sense and learned how to release my anxious feelings with true forgiveness. I let go of my desire to own and control. I took responsibility, in my own mind, for more than I considered my "fair share" of the blame for events. I spent many hours going deeply inward searching for, and finding, peace. I embraced it, fiercely.

I had no choice. The negative feelings of self-loathing were destroying me from the inside out. The lessons had become so painful that it was a matter of survival. Over the years, book after book seemed to fall into my hands, giving me tools to handle this internal crisis. Interesting people and seminars appeared as if by magic and gave me key ideas. My inner attitude steadily improved. I felt better.

My life was still in turmoil, but it didn't bother me as much inside. The anxiety came less frequently and left more quickly. Joy returned. Different than the happiness I knew before, this feeling had no known cause that I could see. It felt wonderful nonetheless. I practiced the exercises that had worked well so far, as negative lessons continued to manifest in my life.

I was still running away from my fears, trying to control events and people and had not embraced trust-in-faith. The idea of one-hundred-percent-responsibility floated in one day and said, "Try this." It was the right idea at the right time. I did it. I didn't blame myself, but I took one hundred percent of the responsibility for everything that happened to me, even if it was clearly not my "fault." It was an epiphany when I realized that *I* was responsible for everything. I accepted that responsibility, internally and completely.

The ideas that are covered in this book were falling into place. They were working! I gave up alcohol. When I felt anxious, I asked for help from my Higher Self, and it was given. The fear subsided quickly, and my faith grew. I suddenly had faith that *everything* was going to be okay. I learned to trust this faith. I saw what my heart of hearts had always known, and I was grateful and deeply humbled to have been given the chance to understand.

This feeling deepened into trust-in-faith and became an unshakable conviction. Life lessons gradually turned positive, and reinforced the right-minded attitude that gave them birth. The clarity that resulted was so peaceful and wise that I felt inspired to write a book about it.

I didn't have to do anything, except change my mind and embrace a different way of thinking. When I really did that, everything changed.

As far as decisions about day-to-day life are concerned, you will come to realize that it doesn't matter what you do as long as you are moving toward your eternal reality (Self). When you line up with that force, your (dream) world shifts to positive and events and people arrive on their own to reinforce the direction. Ideas arrive, too; inspired notions of what you should do next for yourself or for someone else to help them in their life. Creativity is found here. So is health and happiness.

This happens because you have decided, as the Decision Maker, to line up with the Holy Spirit's teaching of forgiveness instead of the ego's message that the dream is real. You have found the place where answers reside, and they have nothing to do with outside conditions. Everything begins and ends within your own mind, with your perceptions, thoughts and feelings. There is no one else, and there need be no one else. All that need be learned is already known, it must just be remembered. Remembering is nothing more than recognizing truth.

> Children perceive frightening ghosts and monsters and dragons, and they are terrified. Yet if they ask someone they trust for the meaning of what they perceive, and are willing to let their own interpretations go in favor of reality, their fear goes with them. When a child is helped to translate his "ghost" into a curtain, his "monster" into a shadow, and his "dragon" into a dream he is no longer afraid, and laughs happily at his own fear.
>
> You, my child, are afraid of your brothers and of your Father and of yourself. But you are merely deceived in them. Ask what they are of the Teacher of reality, and hearing His answer, you too will laugh at your fears and replace them with peace. For fear lies not in reality, but in the minds of children who do not understand reality. It is only their lack of understanding that frightens them, and when they learn to perceive truth they are not afraid. And because of this they will ask for truth again when they are frightened.
>
> —*A Course in Miracles* T-11.VIII.13;1-3,14:1-5

Chapter 12

Atonement and the Holy Instant

For here we come to a decision to accept ourselves as God created us. And what is choice except uncertainty of what we are?
—*A Course in Miracles* W-139.1:2,3

The end of forgiveness is Atonement. Again, in this context, the word does not have a traditional meaning. Atonement in the traditional sense means making amends for past "sins" against others or God with some kind of action. Atonement in the higher sense happens when you are so practiced at forgiveness that it happens naturally all day long in every aspect of your life. You realize that the only sin is thinking that you are a body and the world is real.

The Holy Spirit's message of forgiveness has a powerful cumulative effect over time. Forgiveness is a process and a learning. You learn to employ the process of forgiveness to every area of your life, all the time. You know deep in your being that you are not separate from God, that this world of form is a dream, and you are the dreamer who has never stopped being the one and only Child of God.

This realization comes as a "holy instant" and has nothing to do with your piety. It might happen easily and sometimes quickly, although this is rare. Abraham Maslow, the American psychologist and philosopher, called it a "peak experience" and wrote extensively about the subject.

> Feelings of limitless horizons opening up to the vision, the feeling of being simultaneously more powerful and also more helpless than one ever was before, the feeling of ecstasy and wonder and awe, the loss of placement in time and space with, finally, the conviction that something extremely important and valuable had happened, so that the subject was to some extent transformed and strengthened even in his daily life by such experiences. Peak experiences are sudden feelings of intense happiness and wellbeing, possibly the awareness of an "ultimate truth" and the unity of all things... the experience fills the individual with wonder and awe... he feels at one with the world, and is pleased with it.
>
> —Abraham Maslow

The holy instant is based on willingness: willingness to take the leap of faith and embrace the fact that you are greater than all you have been taught; willingness to surrender yourself to your Self; willingness to surrender judgment and accept the Holy Spirit's guidance.

Atonement is a deep realization, and it comes with almost overwhelming peace and joy. You suddenly understand what "love for your fellow man" means as you recognize at your core that you are everyone and you take it further to include everything.

Your ego still exists, but you see it easily. You know that it is just your fear whispering in your ear. You see that it is ignorant, and you do not judge it as anything other than what it is: your resistance to your eternal reality.

The holy instant happens to you. It is not something that you can "make" happen although truly embracing forgiveness will prepare you to allow it to happen. It is also known as spiritual awakening, waking-up, spiritual enlightenment, reaching nirvana and other names. The holy instant is outside of time and space. It is a shift of perception in which we choose the Holy Spirit instead of the ego, love over fear, in the only time there is, this instant.

> The holy instant is a miniature of eternity. It is a picture of timelessness, set in a frame of time. If you focus on the picture, you will realize that it was only the frame that made you think it was a picture. Without the frame, the picture is seen as what it represents. For as the whole thought system of the ego lies in its gifts, so the whole of Heaven lies in this instant, borrowed from eternity and set in time for you.
>
> —*A Course in Miracles* T-17.IV.11.4-8

> In a moment out of time, your accustomed identity crumbles, and you see beyond the veil of conventional reality to the deeper spiritual ground or undercurrent of existence, of which the material world is merely a manifestation. As a consequence, you can never again view your life in quite the same way, as if it were ultimately real, permanent, or substantial.
>
> —Stephan Bodian

Having experienced the Holy Instant and Atonement in a deeply profound way, Jesus allowed himself to die on the cross to show us in the most convincing way he could that the body is not important compared to who we really are. In so doing he illustrated the lesson that we must allow our attachment to our body (ego) to die in our minds before we will be able to move past the idea of sin and embrace our true magnificence. He died for our sins in the sense that he made the "ultimate sacrifice" as a demonstration of what we must do for ourselves.

We don't have to literally kill our body to prove that we understand this lesson. We merely have to change our mind and understand that we are the Christ, just like Jesus, and we also have the ability to accept Atonement. When we do that, we too will experience a holy instant where we will realize that the only sin we must forgive is our belief that we are separate from God.

The crucifixion symbolizes our behavior in the world. We are all crucifying ourselves with fear. The resurrection is symbolic of our awakening from the dream of crucifixion into love.

There are only two operating principles in the world, love and fear, and of the two, only love is real.

> The god of crucifixion demands that he crucify, and his worshippers obey. In his name they crucify themselves, believing that the power of the Son of God is born of sacrifice and pain. The God of resurrection demands nothing, for He does not will to take away. He does not demand obedience, for obedience implies submission. He would only have you learn your will and follow it, not in the spirit of sacrifice and submission, but in the gladness of freedom.
>
> You who have tried to banish love have not succeeded, but you who choose to banish fear must succeed. The Lord is with you but you know it not.
>
> —*A Course in Miracles* T-11.VI.5;4-8; T-12.II.9;1,2

It is important to understand that Atonement and the holy instant that may accompany it affect very subtle changes in your outward appearance in the "world." If you practice your lessons faithfully and experience the holy instant, it is unlikely that you will become a sage and retire to a cave. You will not gain the ability to see the future and begin prophesying. Your illnesses will not heal miraculously, and you will gain no extra-ordinary abilities. You will still need to eat and breathe and work for a living.

Your perception changes radically, however, and this may cause changes in how you choose to live your life. Negative ego emotions like anger, arrogance and greed become repugnant in yourself, and you might start to avoid people who exhibit them. You might become more giving and donate time to help others. If your job requires that you engage in duplicity or harm to other people you will probably not be able to continue doing it. You will smile more. You will see other people as the beautiful spirit they are, and notice but not judge them by their ego anymore. You may become so comfortable alone with yourself that your friends might ask where you have been. Your anxious worries will fade to mere concerns that seem to solve themselves.

As you make progress on the path, these changes will slowly incorporate themselves into your thoughts and affect the way you spend your time. When the awakening occurs, the additional changes that happen are slight and pertain more to your inner feelings than to the way you act, the things you do or what you say, because most external changes have already happened.

Atonement and the holy instant are internal realizations that release fear and embrace love. They apply to your thoughts and your feelings. They affect behavior because they change your judgments and free you from the slavery of your egoic thoughts and desires. When this happens, you see clearly and act lovingly. Your mind is peaceful. You are serene inside. You may accomplish great things, if that is your disposition, or you may simply enjoy being. Your co-workers and acquaintances won't notice anything is different, and your friends will only know if you tell them. You will be the same external person you have always been, just happier, more peaceful, less prone to mishaps and the "lucky" recipient of positive lessons that validate your confidence in your chosen path.

Chapter 13

Afterlife

> *When your body and your ego and your dreams are gone, you will know that you will last forever. Perhaps you think this is accomplished through death, but nothing is accomplished through death, because death is nothing. Everything is accomplished through life, and life is of the mind and in the mind. The body neither lives nor dies, because it cannot contain you who are life.*
>
> —*A Course in Miracles*, T.6.V.A.1:1- 4

What happens when our body dies? Why did we have to live in the first place?

Most people think that all their questions will be answered when their body dies and they sally forth to collect their eternal reward. Nothing could be further from the truth.

Just as the real "you" isn't living here in the physical world but merely dreaming that you are, "you" cannot die either. Your body will eventually expire in your dream, but the dream will continue. So will your ego. Your perspective changes, nothing more.

More than twenty years ago, Dr. Brian Weiss embarked on groundbreaking work involving past lives, which he continues to explore through a (now) recognized therapy known as hypno-regression.

For those who may not have heard of him, Dr. Weiss is a Yale-trained psychiatrist who stumbled onto the fact of past lives and their effect on our current life with a patient under his care. The effectiveness of this therapy on his patient's life was so startling, so rapid, and so unexpected that he risked ridicule and banishment from his profession to write a book about it. *Many Lives Many Masters* is now a classic, and he continues to write books about his experiences with this therapy. Far from being laughed out of the university, his research was embraced by the majority of his fellow professors who described events in their own lives that reinforced his conclusion that we (meaning our soul) live hundreds if not thousands of lives.

These lives are accessible to everyone but best explored under hypnosis with a trained professional, of which there are many now in practice throughout the world. There are literally thousands of success stories in which a patient is able to release an irrational fear, control a formerly uncontrollable urge, or make peace with another individual by simply "remembering" an event that happened in a past life that caused the issue. It continues to be an unorthodox but respected therapeutic technique.

We can glean from this work that our consciousness is only connected to our body as long as our body remains alive, and after that it moves on. Where it goes in between lives and why it chooses any particular next life is the subject of Dr. Michael Newton's forty-year study, again using hypno-regression with his patients.

These books are fascinating to say the least, and the reader can explore them in their entirety. Both author's works are readily available at most bookstores and have been translated into many other languages.

Near death experiences (NDEs) are another popular area of inquire into our soul's journey after life. *Saved by the Light* by Dannion Brinkley and *Life After Life* by Dr. Raymond Moody reveal numerous case studies of people who have literally died, sometimes for many minutes as in the case of Mr. Brinkley, but return to tell surprisingly similar stories of our life between lives. Common themes of a tunnel opening to a bright light, angelic beings of light and the dearly departed awaiting us, life reviews and a sense of peace so profound that most report being very reluctant to return. Almost every person who experiences such phenomena is changed for the better and some even gain extraordinary perceptions.

The documented NDE cases number in the tens of thousands these days and the "evidence" seems hard to deny. It seems quite clear that our consciousness continues after the demise of our physical body.

We are not going to get deeply into the subject of past lives except to understand where they fit as part of our reality as the one Child of God. The exploration of the soul's journey is by no means unimportant and an understanding of it is recommended, but strict adherents run the risk of stopping far short of a complete understanding of who we really are.

Both of the good doctors mentioned above as well as the authors of books on near death studies will readily admit that their work does not explain the nature of reality and why we exist in the first place and where we are going. So let's see if we can take it to the next level.

We have already established that we are not our bodies, we are not our thoughts, and we are not even our soul. Remember, our soul contains us so it can't *be* us.

We are the Christ who is having a dream that she is separate from God. In the dream, our ego has convinced us that the world is real and we have accepted that without question. We have listened to our earthly teachers who have told us that the Lord is a good shepherd or a jealous God (take your pick) who will either punish us or reward us after our body dies based on how we behaved when our body was alive. Some version of this story is our collective theological dream, or nightmare.

We can choose to participate in this story and listen to the ego, or we can embrace the Holy Spirit's message of forgiveness and seek our true reality.

Those who do not move forward into their right mind reward the ego and condemn themselves to doing it over again. That's okay. There is no hurry. We never left God in the first place, so if the dream continues for a few more lifetimes it is of little consequence.

If there is no "physical" life except in our minds (because we, as the Christ, are having a dream that we are separate from the Father), then there is no "after" life either, except in our minds.

This is not to say that the afterlife in all of its marvelous complexity isn't just as real as our physical life. According to sources above, it is even more spectacular and a testament to the depths to which the ego will go to convince us that we are indeed separate from God. We aren't separate from God. We never have been, and no matter how many lives we lead, we never will be.

We are on a quest together. We came from the same place, we share a common Awareness, and we will all find our way home to the place we never left. It cannot be anything else and everything else is an ego trap, including the afterlife in all of its intricacy.

Sorry. You didn't really think it could be anything else, did you?

So why do we have to live in the first place?

The short answer is that we aren't living, we're having a dream. But you know that already. I know you know that.

The long answer is that we are experiencing the dream in the physical world because it has a much greater potential for advancement than any other plane of existence for us at our current level of spiritual development.

The physical allows for extremes of experience that are not possible elsewhere. This can have a profound effect on our growth. In other words, it is harder here with the potential for "death" lurking around every corner. This lends an air of urgency and requires a level of faith that is not possible in the "afterlife." We chose to be here for that reason. We aren't any more "all knowing" after death than we are during life, but we do know beyond a shadow of a doubt that we continue after the death of the physical body. This takes away some of the faith that is so important for progress.

The lessons here are more poignant. We feel them more intensely. We are very aware of our mortality, and we burn with a desire that isn't possible anywhere else. We come to our lives with a set of goals that we hope will help us advance. We set up it ahead of time in a calculated attempt to move forward. We are actively working to get back to the place we started, and if we don't know where it is while we are alive we won't have any better idea in the afterlife. We do continue our "work" in between lives but in order to make more progress we incarnate into a body and live yet another physical life that we hope will move us forward.

So cherish the fact that you had the courage to come here and that you have given yourself this opportunity to grow. It took tremendous courage. If you are reading this, chances are that you have a life that affords time for contemplation. Don't squander it pursuing ego goals and don't think that that your experience beyond the body will be enlightening in the ultimate sense beyond what you have been able to attain so far.

Chapter 14

The Mirror

It is a common characteristic of human nature that a man sees the faults of others more easily than he sees his own. At the same time on the path of self-study he learns that he himself possesses all the faults that he finds in others. In order to see himself in other people's faults and not merely to see the faults of others, a man must be very sincere with himself.

—George Ivanovich Gurdjieff

So how does one "not squander" their life pursuing ego goals? The concept of the "mirror" is one of the more helpful ideas.

We all lead busy lives. We are involved in them deeply, and we seem to have nary a second to spare for contemplation. Luckily, we don't have to shut ourselves away and think deep thoughts in order to make startling progress along the path or even to achieve enlightenment in this lifetime.

Our "world" is a projection that we made because we listened to the ego and believed we were separate from each other and God. But our world is also a classroom with the Holy Spirit as the teacher. We choose which one we want to have as our reality every second of every day. Most of us have our feet firmly planted in the ego's camp, but with a little practice and a new way of looking at things we can begin to use the effects of the dream to propel ourselves into the Holy Spirit's camp. When this begins to happen, there is no doubt because it feels wonderful and we naturally embrace a deep sense of faith born from trust.

When you start to listen to your heart of hearts, also known as the Holy Spirit, the effect on your life is noticeable. Your temperament improves as you become aligned with who you really are. The real you is a serenely peaceful, indescribably joyful, ultimately patient, fundamentally grateful, humble, generous being of Love. When you touch your Higher Self these feelings flow into you. You know they are real because they are not fleeting or dependent on any outside conditions. They are not hollow, and they radiate in a way that is perceptible to others, who are drawn to you just because it feels good to be in your presence.

Everything that you perceive in the world is but a projection of yourself. You made it up so you could escape, but it is really you, and every other person whom you encounter is a mirror of you. It is as if the universe (you) created a way for you to see where you are along the path to enlightenment.

Enlightenment is what happens when you touch your Higher Self, learn to listen to the Holy Spirit or become aware of your heart of hearts to the point that they are with you in your conscious mind all the time. You know in every fiber of your being that you are one with all and that the real "you" exists outside of time in blissful communion with your eternal reality. You do not define it because it cannot be defined. You live in the holy instant with a calm certitude and watch events and even your own actions unfold in the dream as if they were merely a projection on a screen.

Most people think that they are separate from everyone else, and they are not responsible for the actions or attitudes of others. They know that if they behave badly they can expect some repercussions (which they may even believe they deserve), but almost no one truly believes that other people are a projection of themselves. Yet that is exactly what they are. You are everyone, and everyone is you. We have already established this in numerous ways earlier in the book.

The best way to touch your Higher Self is by practicing true forgiveness in all areas of your life, to ask the Holy Spirit for help as you do it, and to clear your mind during meditation so that you are open to the flow of peace, love, and inspiration. It is important to realize that other people are here to help you succeed in your mission to embrace your eternal reality, although it may not seem that way at first.

The feelings that other people engender in you are "mirrors" of your internal condition at that moment. They reflect you to you. Although this is true of all people, the most instructive reflections will come from those with whom you have a significant relationship. This is what makes relationships so hard. We steadfastly refuse to believe that significant others are *ourselves* in reality. When the other person does or says something that we don't like or that offends us or makes us feel abandoned, smothered, or any emotion besides peace and love, it is a reflection of a wrong-minded attitude that we projected onto the other person that needs correction within ourselves. Our inner condition is on full display *to us* as we look at our private reactions to the words and actions of significant people in our lives.

You choose your reactions! You can choose to be annoyed and resentful and blame others for your feelings. You are embracing the ego when you do this, and it is *never* helpful. You had that negative feeling inside you before the incident happened, and you were just waiting for an excuse to project it out. This is your resistance to your heritage operating smoothly to keep you trapped in the dream.

When angry or anxious feelings arise, no matter how justified they seem, it is a significant opportunity to ask for help from the

Holy Spirit (or Jesus or Buddha or God or your Higher Self) to understand that this *is* the ego at work and nothing more. The ego wants you to believe that the problem is with the other person and not in you! Those angry feelings can be forgiven. They *can* be released and never return. After you have sincerely forgiven the person and spent at least five minutes on the activity, you can actually shift over to the Holy Spirit's camp and feel love and kindness flow in to you. This change can be rapid, and it feels like the release it is. It feels like you just broke through a barrier, almost like a runner's high. Suddenly you are coasting on love's wings, and you know in your heart that everything is going to be okay because the only problem was within you. Now that it's gone, you can see that!

Unhappy feelings like anxiety, anger, jealousy and the like are just thoughts gone astray. When we are in the middle of them, we believe (for some absurd reason) that we will always think this way and the feelings are going to be with us forever. We know this isn't the case of course, but we act as if it is true. We give those thoughts power by thinking them, and the ego loves it because we are projecting into the dream and making it very real.

No matter how real they seem, they are just thoughts and they will go away on their own sooner or later. Forgiveness is a wonderfully effective way to feel better faster. Another excellent way to avoid negative thoughts, and the mirror they represent, is through the practice of compassion.

Compassion is a way to look beyond the behavior to the source of it. When you can see the cause of someone else's distress, you react with understanding and love rather than becoming defensive or acting in kind. Compassion does not judge but sees beyond the superficial aspects of the language, the demeanor, and the actions to the real motivation that is causing them.

For instance, a person in your life might criticize your parenting skills. Rather than reacting "in ego" and being hurt, embarrassed, angry and lashing out, a compassionate person will see that the real motivation for making such an accusation comes from a feeling of insecurity, maybe about their own parenting abilities. Usually the cause is not too hard to see if you look for it instead of focusing on what was said or done. Maybe they are jealous. The compassionate person will hear the criticism and then may think about how sad it is that the other person feels so poorly about themselves that they have to condemn others in an attempt to feel better. Compassion sees the scared little boy who was abused by his father in the eyes of the man who strikes his son.

A compassionate reaction results in a clear-headed feeling of understanding and caring, not a muddy-headed defensive, emotional reaction. When we are clear and compassionate, we say and do things that dissipate the negative situation. Maybe we make a self deprecating joke or simply ask the person if they are okay. Compassion sees through the situation and projects warmth from the core. When love and understanding are projected, they cannot help but be reflected back. It might not happen at that moment, but the speed with which it does happen can be surprising.

Sometimes there is a grain of truth in the offensive comment or a lesson that should be taken to heart in a less-than-kind action. Compassionate thinking keeps the mind clear and allows humility and wisdom to rise and handle the situation. This is our natural state. It is only the ego (our fearful self) that keeps us pinned to painful thoughts and resentful actions.

If you feel warm and safe with important people in your life and you feel comfortable and open when you communicate with them, and you do not judge yourself as superior or inferior, and their perceptions of you are not dependant on anything that you do or are, then you have tapped into your compassion and are projecting your essential nature as one with all in that group.

Don't mistake a lack of conflict for true peace, however. Lack of conflict may be a temporary ego condition that merely reflects a lull in its pursuit of trials that keep you focused outward. It is a false positive. You know it is false because your heart of hearts will tell you, if you ask, that the only reason you have "peace" is because you have dropped the conflict. You have not released it. You are just biding your time. You may give lip service to releasing and even try to fool yourself, but you have not done it if the other person or your thoughts about a particular situation can revive those negative feelings.

True peace is palpable. It pulses through your veins. Our mind is joyful and clear and our outward attitude is quiet and subdued because we know we have nothing to prove. To achieve and maintain true peace, we must direct our thoughts there every time we have the opportunity. We want to do this, and it begins to happen naturally. Our inner world becomes a place we like to be, and we go there a lot. We never neglect our responsibilities but allow our Higher Self to be our partner as we listen to the Holy Spirit before deciding on our course of action. When this begins to happen, you will recognize it, and you will know that it is unlike any feeling you have had previously in your life.

Listening to the Holy Spirit does not mean that we close our eyes and consult it before making any decisions. The world is a classroom, and everything that we think, say or do falls into two areas: ego thoughts and actions and Higher Self thoughts and actions. As we move around in the classroom with honest awareness of this fact, we will see them more and more clearly. Then we ask for help to release the ego thoughts and actions.

That's all we have to do. If we do it sincerely, it happens. If we allow our natural feelings of love and peace to arise by thinking compassionate thoughts, they will!

No one is born connected to peace. Everyone who achieves it has consciously looked for it until they found it and nurtured peace into a presence in their lives. They maintain their peaceful attitude by not giving negative thoughts the time and attention they seem to want.

You have many internal conflicts, and you receive different reflections from different people. You may be feeling anxiety with your spouse, but your relationship with your father feels calm and safe. These "mirrors" may have been reversed just a short time ago. Both are you, and both reflect your inner condition at that time. If you examine your thoughts, you may find that you are giving one person the "benefit of the doubt" but holding another responsible for every perceived inflection, grimace, and sigh. Try to give everyone the benefit of the doubt. You don't have to agree with what they say to be able to listen with this attitude of openness. The attitude itself is all that is necessary to create a positive reflection.

The mirror always points inside. Anxiety is just as internal as peace. They are opposite poles of our inner self; one is just "wrong minded" and needs forgiveness, the other is "right minded" and should be encouraged. Giving others the benefit of the doubt and looking past the issue to the cause with compassion will encourage right-minded thinking and place our thoughts in alignment with the Holy Spirit's message of forgiveness.

Strong feelings are always triggered by other people. Because of these wonderful signposts, we are able to identify those areas that require forgiveness. But we do it all within ourselves. After we have forgiven the person for what they did not do and released it in our mind, we are ready to communicate with them and talk about the issues.

We forgive people for what they did not do for two reasons. First, because they and the world are a dream that you are having, whatever they did, did not "really" happen. "They" didn't do anything because "they" are a manifestation of "you." You did it to yourself.

Second, since you are the only one who can create anxiety or fear within yourself and you are the only one who can release it, other people did not do anything to you. They do not have the power to create emotions within you. If you think they do, you are falling into the ego's trap of believing the outside world has the ability to affect your inner condition. It doesn't. The outside world merely *reflects* our inside world. If we change our inner world, the outer will naturally follow.

Our inner condition is mostly subconscious, so changing it isn't as simple as being told this fact. It takes practice and mind training. Our subconscious mind is the part of the iceberg that is under water—the part we cannot see. It is, however, the part that drives all the reflections in our life. Thoughts are infinitely powerful because we are the Christ who has forgotten his true heritage. Change your subconscious thoughts, and you change your life.

So how do you consciously change your unconscious ego thoughts?

First, you recognize the truth behind the concept that you are the dreamer and the world can be used as a classroom to help you internalize this concept. You agree with it completely. You think about the fact that you are not separate from God and that you are more like Jesus' or Buddha's brother than some simple soul who must worship great deities.

You think of yourself as the one Child of God who is having a dream for the experience of it and *nothing* more. You try hard every day to see the world as a great big interactive holodeck except that all the people in it are really you. It's an unfamiliar thought system to be sure, but it is not incomprehensible or impossible to begin to think this way. Using these thoughts, you begin to train your mind to think differently: to think in a way that taps into the real "you"; to completely understand consciously what you want to embody subconsciously. Over time, it will begin to happen.

Consciously employing compassion and giving everyone the benefit of the doubt is the best way to stop the ego in its tracks and embrace your Higher Self. Your Higher Self and all those wonderful warm loving thoughts are the real "you." The ego represents your fear of those loving thoughts. If you practice it, a compassionate response will become second nature. It can become the easiest of all the concepts to internalize and employ in your daily thoughts, actions, and conversations with others.

Anything that causes fear, anxiety, jealousy, anger, envy, guilt or any negative emotion is a mirror of an issue that needs to be released within you. When something *outside* causes an unpleasant feeling *inside*, it is an indication of a release point. This is an opportunity to practice forgiveness in the classroom of life.

If you do not release the issue in this way, it will return in a different guise again and again in your world. This is because your spiritual progress in this area has hit a snag and you cannot move forward until you release it through forgiveness. We all have issues that seem to come up repeatedly in our relationships, or our work, or our health. It seems that no sooner is one problem solved than another similar one takes its place and the cycle continues. Sometimes years separate the same lesson, but you recognize it immediately and wonder, *Why, oh why, is this happening again?* The reason is that "you" are giving yourself another opportunity to release and move forward; an opportunity to forgive truly and completely by letting go and surrendering control to your Higher Self through trust. Your Higher Self (the real you) is teaching the little you a lesson from an eternal perspective, and you can either embrace it and learn, or muddle through and have it come back later. Many times the lesson is as simple as learning compassion. Once compassion is embraced, you will find that many of your formerly negative mirrors turn positive.

Once truly released, the issue need not recur because you have learned this lesson and can move on to the next one. The lessons never stop, because life is one big classroom where everything is a lesson. They can turn positive, however, as you surrender control to trust and embrace peace and joy. These positive attributes reinforce your progress and keep you moving forward because they attract good things into your life. When the little problem recurs you are better prepared to forgive and let go, which soon renders it unnecessary and you suffer very little. The proof is so visceral that once you begin to understand what is happening, you may actually welcome little problems as the opportunity they are and rush to forgive them gladly, knowing that you can do it and they really can go away and never return!

You will know that you have successfully released a recurring issue (forgiven it) when the issue crops up again but it does not engender an emotional reaction within your body either positive or negative. Your body is a wonderful indicator of a release point. When you have a noticeable emotional reaction to events or people within your body, such as anxiety or jealousy or anger, it is an unmistakable indication that a release point is near and forgiveness is possible. The action of truly letting the feeling go (forgiving it) in your heart and calming your body's reaction will result in releasing the issue. It may take numerous tries with the same issue, but it will get easier. You will calm down faster each time. Then one time the issue will happen, and you will feel no reaction to it in your body. You will still have to deal with it, but your mind will be clear and calm and you will resolve the problem efficiently. Soon it will stop coming up, or when it does it will be such a non-issue that you will not think of it as a serious problem anymore even though it used to cause real distress and a noticeable physical reaction. It will actually become hard to remember that that issue ever was a real problem for you.

Remember, you forgive by telling yourself that whatever happened isn't "real." It is just your ego laying a trap to make you believe that the world is not a dream. Ask the Holy Spirit for help to embrace the fact that the real you is the one Child of God and every distressing thing that happens here is nothing more than a momentary fantasy with no other purpose than to support the ego. Feel for the release within your body and allow it to happen. Let whatever is bothering you go. Practice every day to see all difficulties as nothing more than the ego working hard to keep you trapped.

This doesn't mean that you don't take corrective action or endeavor to accomplish a goal that is being elusive. It means that you do not experience an unproductive *internal emotional reaction* to the recurring problem. When you no longer have this kind of reaction, the issue is forgiven. Even though it may return, it becomes a shadow that vanishes in the light.

One-time events that cause very strong, painful emotional reactions must also be released. In the same way that certain smaller life issues recur so you can forgive them slowly and methodically, major life issues happen in one big burst and continue or tail off (internally and emotionally) based on how well you can forgive them and let them go.

When you get upset because you didn't get what your ego thinks it deserves at work or your financial investments lose money, it is probably a recurring issue that will benefit from repeated release exercises and striving to embrace compassion. When tragedy strikes and you injure yourself, harm another, or get terribly sick, someone close to you dies, you lose your job, or your marriage crumbles, this can be thought of as a one-time event. Your internal emotional reaction will be much more powerful and longer in duration.

When that emotional reaction rises up in your body, take a mental "time out" and find a way to center yourself and regain your emotional balance. Remind yourself that none of that transpired in the eternal sense, and try to *forgive* it. Tell yourself that these things happen to keep you trapped in the dream of thinking that you are separate from God, and remind yourself that you are one with all. This traumatic "lesson" is a big opportunity for forward progress. With a recurring issue, an issue similar to one that happened in the past recurs, and with it, the negative feeling. With a one-time issue the negative *feeling* recurs due to your memory of the event. Either way the process of forgiveness is the same.

One-time issues can be excruciatingly painful, and release does not mean that you won't feel sadness or be upset. You will. It doesn't mean you shouldn't make amends if you make a mistake and hurt another. You should. Admit (inside yourself) that you are a "student" and ask for help from your inner guide for inspiration to do what is best. Then forgive it to the best of your ability by letting go and releasing the *feeling* to your Higher Self.

When a loved one dies unexpectedly we miss them (sometimes terribly) and feel intense sadness that they are no longer with us in the world. When we find ourselves in difficult situations, we get anxious. This is natural, and to deny it won't help. You don't have to deny how you feel to be able to put the situation into a higher perspective in your mind, however. We will explore how to forgive and truly release our feelings to our Higher Self next in the chapter on meditation and active prayer. Once the process has been understood and internalized, it can be employed when it is needed any time of the day or night.

You know, in your heart of hearts, that all negative feelings, no matter how powerful, are temporary. You know that you will eventually move past whatever trials life brings, no matter how tragic. If you want to do it more peacefully and prevent recurrence, you will learn to forgive the trials by recognizing that they are ego traps even as you grieve and work to set your life back on track.

Once you have forgiven the person for what they did not do and released the feeling to the best of your ability, move your thoughts away from it! Read a book. Think about a wonderful experience that you had or are planning. Call a friend and talk about something different than your issue of the moment. Do not let the ego invade your mind with endless thoughts of unproductive worry, regret, guilt or anger. When that happens, recognize it and shift your thoughts.

Many problems require discussion with others, but try, if possible, to have the conversation after you have released most of the anxiety. Do not make a habit of escaping into activities that merely postpone the worry or the conflict, such as watching television, playing video games or indulging in alcohol or drugs. If you use these activities to escape, they have become part of the problem and you have succumbed to ego's siren song.

Remember, it isn't what happens to you on the outside. Everyone on the planet experiences difficulties and tragedy. It is how you deal with these things on the inside that makes all the difference. You choose how you perceive your life. There may seem to be hundreds of choices, but there are only two: the ego or the Holy Spirit. If you choose the ego, you condemn yourself to misery, pain and hopes that are consistently dashed. It you choose the Holy Spirit and use the world as a classroom to practice your forgiveness lessons, you will experience peace and joy that are not dependant on external conditions. Your world will fall into alignment with your thinking, and good things will start to happen to you. This works because your outer world *always* mirrors your inner condition.

> When you can identify with the purpose of changing your mind and teacher, your life from birth to death, from the time you wake up to the time you go to sleep, will have great meaning. You will close your eyes at night with a sense of fulfillment, not necessarily because you learned all there was to learn, but because you understood your life in the world is a classroom—neither prison nor paradise. You rest easily with the thought that even if you had not learned all your lessons, tomorrow is yet another day, taught by a teacher who is infinitely patient. Thus you awake each morning with joy and return joyfully to bed at night, regardless of the day's perceived successes or failures, for you have identified with the only purpose that makes life meaningful.
>
> —Kenneth Wapnick

Chapter 15

Meditation and Active Prayer

Meditation opens wide all the closed inner doors of your body, mind and soul to admit the surge of God's power. Your entire body and entire being changes when you practice meditation regularly. Contact with God brings inner harmony to your life as you merge with His peace. But you must meditate earnestly, consistently, and continually to realize fully the rewarding effects of that Supreme force.

—Paramhansa Yogananda

Time for quiet contemplation is so important. To calm the mind and open the spirit is a natural ability that everyone has. Most people do not know this, so they do not take time to pray or meditate in any meaningful manner.

Some are actually afraid of meditating, fearing that their thoughts will turn on them and devour them in an orgy of guilt, regret and worry. They run from their fear of these thoughts and fill their waking moments with a constant stream of stimuli, whether it is conversation, work, activities or electronic escape.

There is nothing wrong with working and thinking about how to do it best. There is nothing wrong with watching a movie or playing a game. Conversation can be very beneficial (unless it is negative towards another), and we all have obligations we must fulfill. It is using these activities as an escape from our thoughts (fears) that causes problems to develop in our life.

Spending time alone quietly communing with your Self is the best way to loosen the knots that the ego tied in your thoughts as you allow true peace to untangle, unravel and release your fears.

Far from being a time when your ego takes you to task for all of your real or imagined past blunders and feeds your insecurity about the what is to come, both prayer and meditation become a time that you use to establish and fortify your connection with your true reality as the Christ and reach out to your own divine nature.

Of course you could use the time to ruminate about the past and worry about the future and surrender to all of your ego fears, but if you had a choice, why would you want to do that? You do have a choice. You can direct your thoughts. You can focus on the task at hand and let all other thoughts and concerns wait until you are ready to entertain them.

Prayer and meditation are very similar. Both are done either alone or in a group. Both can be self-directed or guided. Time is set aside and concerns are put away until the contemplation is over.

Prayer is when you ask the Holy Spirit or Jesus or Buddha or God or your Higher Self for help to accomplish your forgiveness lessons. It is the only prayer that can be granted because it is the only prayer that asks for something that makes a real difference as you travel along the road to Atonement. You ask for help to forgive yourself for what you did not do and pray for help to forgive others for what they did not do. You place your earthly problems in the hands of God as a token of your faith in the fact that they are not real, compared to your true reality as one with all that is.

Do not pray for things or outcomes to events, even if these outcomes seem altruistic, like world peace or health for the sick. These are not prayers that God can grant. To ask for them presumes that you know best and confirms that you think the illusion is "real." Pray for inspiration to take action that will result in an outcome that is best for all concerned. We are all moving along the path together, and this prayer confirms that we do not know what is the best result and affirms our faith that we will be guided to a positive conclusion even if we don't know how or when or why.

The positive conclusion is, of course, the one that leads us closer to our eternal reality. Misery, sickness, pain, tragedy and even death may help accomplish this. Our role is not to judge but merely accept with faith that this is happening for a good reason and work internally on our only purpose, which is to achieve Atonement. This may indeed lead to many external activities. The activities that we feel inspired to engage will always be those that bring us closer to our immortal reality. They happen easily. Even if they require a great deal of energy, we feel refreshed.

Meditation is when you listen for inspiration, feel true peace, experience joy and recognize your Self as a being of love. It can be done before, during or after prayer. In the beginning it is best to separate the two activities in your mind and consciously focus your thoughts on one or the other. Later you will be able to engage in both during the same period of contemplation.

What follows is an example of active prayer. This is just an example. There are as many ways of doing it as there are people on the earth. Certain basic goals should be accomplished to make the experience effective, and those are clearly illuminated below. Beyond that the practice is up to you, your imagination and your Higher Self.

When you are ready to pray or meditate, set some time aside for the activity. Half an hour is a good place to start. Pick a time when you are not likely to be interrupted, like early in the morning or later in the evening. Find a comfortable place to sit. This can be a chair or couch or the floor on a pillow. You can play soft music or do it in silence. The lights can be on or you can be in the dark. Maybe a candle seems like a good idea. Straighten your back, put your head up with the chin facing out, and place your hands on your lap with the palms facing up in a gesture of openness.

Close your eyes and focus your attention on the spot between your eyebrows. This is known as your spiritual eye. If you notice pressure or a "crinkling" feeling in this spot as you meditate that is a good sign. It means you are relaxed and open to your awareness of your Higher Self.

Take a deep breath in, pulling from your diaphragm, as you allow your abdomen to expand before your chest and pull the air deep into your lungs through your nose. Release this "cleansing breath" through your mouth. Take another cleansing breath and push it out. Take a third if you like. All other breaths can be released through your nose or you can continue to exhale through your mouth. All inhalations should come through the nose. You are ready to begin.

Start by consciously relaxing your body. You may want to begin with your brow and feel it unfurrow. Next move to your eyeballs. Consciously relax your eyeballs, then your jaw then your neck. Imagine the tension leaving these areas on your breath as you exhale. Allow your breath to carry away any tension in your shoulders, your back, your chest. Move your attention to each body part and relax that area before moving to the next. In this way move slowly and consciously from your head to your toes. Think only of relaxing each area as you breathe in, and allow out-flowing air to carry your tension, your stress and your thoughts away.

Consciously relax your brain. That great and mighty organ inside your skull that is helping you calm down and connect. Give your brain permission to slow down and feel it respond. Feel the stress leave your brain as your thoughts assume less urgency. Let your brain have no thoughts. Just breathe and relax.

Feel your heart beating. Feel the steady rush of blood pulsing through your body. Feel your "alive-ness." Open your heart. Symbolically remove the shield you may have placed around your heart by pulling your shoulders back from their protective position. Push your heart forward in a gesture of openness and vulnerability and trust. Breathe and relax.

If a thought comes in, that's okay. Notice it and move it gently out of your mind. If you notice that you are thinking about something, that's okay, too. Just stop thinking those thoughts, move them gently aside and return to concentrating on your breathing. Think, "iiinnn" on the inhale and "ooouuuttt" on the exhale.

After you have relaxed your body and calmed your mind, take some time to move yourself into a deep state of relaxation. If it helps, imagine yourself walking down a staircase where each step you take moves you deeper and deeper into yourself. As thoughts come in, move them aside and continue to breathe in and out as you step deeper and deeper into total relaxation and peace. Focus your attention on your spiritual eye, but don't try to train your eyes on that spot. Just focus your attention there. Watch the colors and the texture of the inside of your eyelids. See the swirls and allow that dizzy fuzzy feeling to arise and envelope you. When you reach the end of the stairway, you are ready to pray or simply be. You decide.

If you are going to pray, begin by imagining that your Higher Self is a wise being who is with you and create a surrounding for you both to occupy. Maybe it is garden or a beach or a field of flowers. Realize that the wise being is the Holy Spirit, your Higher Self—your memory of your Self as the one and only Child of God. Confirm with her (or him) that your reality as the Christ is the only thing that is real, and tell her your earthly problems. Ask for her help to forgive those issues and release them to her. Ask for help to let them go. Ask for help to truly forgive them. Admit that you are not very good at letting go, but promise to try with her help.

Remember the feeling of the negative emotion that the problem created in you when it first happened or as it happens when you think about it. Let that feeling (the one the problem causes in you) pass from you to her, and imagine her gratefully accepting it as a gift of trust that she will handle from now on. Ask for inspiration if you should do something more and have confidence that she will cause the best thing to happen for all concerned if there is nothing more that you should do.

Then move on to your next problem and repeat the process. You may want to change your surroundings as you move to different issues. Imagine yourselves at the edge of a cliff then surrender the problem and walk back from the brink together. If different surroundings arise on their own, go with them. If she leads you, follow. Sit, stand, walk, fly or float in the air—whatever feels right to give over the problem and ask for help is okay. Just try to stay on task with the objective of prayer, which is surrendering to the truth that nothing is "real" except God. Ask for help to realize that fact in the deepest core of your being.

When you are done, rest for a moment and bask in the glow that surrounds you. Then move to the stairs and walk (or fly if you like) to the top. Take a final cleansing breath, open your eyes, and return to your world of form.

The above is just an example. The objectives should be clear. The most effective emotion to bring is willingness. Be willing to confirm your belief in your Self as one with all that is, and willingly reaffirm your conviction that nothing is "real" except this fact. Willingly affirm your commitment to learning to forgive. Communicate your trust that everything will be okay if you leave it in the hands of your Almighty Self. Withdraw your ego-need to control the outcome and let go willingly. Ask for help to do this. Admit that you have trouble. Give your problem of the moment to your Higher Self viscerally by allowing the memory of the negative feeling to flow from you to your Self. Imagine it accepted gratefully as the token of trust that it is. Ask for inspiration and for faith.

If this the first time you have prayed like this and it feels contrived, that's okay. You are probably used to praying for things or desired outcomes, and you finish up with a prayer you have memorized and no real feeling that your prayers were heard or that anything will be all right. You are probably used to hoping that God will grant your wishes as if He were more like a genie than the Creator of all.

As you practice this new way of praying for forgiveness and release and find new ways to transfer your negative feelings to your Higher Self, it will begin to feel more real than any other kind of prayer. You will come back from your time with your Self knowing that inspiration and opportunity will arrive when you need to act and that the best thing will always happen. As you realize that you do not know what is best for all, you will stop trying to control events and be more accepting of what actually transpires. You will realize that there are no "bad" outcomes, only outcomes for which you do not understand the reason. How could it be any other way?

Let's say you decide to meditate instead of pray. Below is another example. Feel free to change any of the situations and characters. They are not important. The important part is to not allow worries of the day to intrude and to encourage the feelings of connectedness and peace to arise.

Meditation is true quiet time. It is the time when you focus on your breathing and allow your mind to grow calm. It is the time when you open to your Higher Self and reach toward the Presence that is so near and only waiting for your call. It is an activity of feeling. Your Greater Self is always with you. It *is* you, in fact. This "real" part of you is merely drowned out by your thoughts and the ego's shrill insistence.

Meditation is the time to allow your Higher Self to surround you and comfort you with your true heritage. Surrender to his (or her) presence and simply enjoy how good it feels. Wait for inspiration, and if it is to come it will. If it doesn't, that is okay, too. Enjoy the moment and let the positive feelings flow into you and around you. Allow time to stop. You will return soon enough to the world of trials, the classroom of forgiveness and all your obligations. For now, however, just relax and be confident that this time you spend with the Self who is not separate from God cannot help but have a positive impact on your life.

After you have relaxed your entire body as above and deepened the feeling by walking down a staircase or rising in a balloon higher and higher as you go deeper and deeper inside yourself and into relaxation, imagine that you have arrived at place like the garden mentioned above, or a big fluffy cloud that pulsates with peaceful feelings. Or, maybe you'd enjoy floating softly over to a field of flowers and drifting gently onto the petals and allowing the aroma to permeate your being with a beautiful feeling of pure peace.

Once you are in that peaceful place and thinking nothing but a gentle "iiinnn" as you breathe in and "ooouuuttt" as you breathe out, begin to open your heart. Place your attention on the right side of your chest, which is the seat of your spiritual heart, and think about your spirit opening up as if it were the bud of a rose opening to the sun. Breathe slowly and rhythmically in and out as you open more and more. Allow a peaceful feeling to come in. Welcome it. Feel it softly and tentatively touch your being and slowly envelop you in a warm wonderful cocoon of blissful peace.

Feel the peace sooth your worries and allow it to penetrate as deep as you can. Experience how warm and wonderful it feels. Have no thoughts. Just enjoy. Breathe slowly in and out as the peace becomes more and more a part of you.

Be open to inspiration but not to idle thoughts. Don't rehash your worries or allow a thought you have had before. These are ego thoughts, and they would love to enter and destroy your peace. Move them gently out of your mind and continue to feel the peace and think only about your breathing.

If you can, allow the peaceful feelings to get stronger. As they get stronger, allow yourself to realize that this is a little taste what you truly are. This peaceful, worry-free feeling is what your Higher Self feels all the time. Be happy and grateful that you have been able to experience it, and wish that you could share it with everyone.

Do exactly that if you want, and share it with everyone you know starting with anyone with whom you are having a conflict. Imagine the peace you feel moving into their being and surrounding them in a soft bubble of peaceful love.

Remind yourself that they are you and that by sharing your peace you are helping yourself. Don't do it for personal gain.

Do it from love of your Greater Self with the knowledge that their happiness is your happiness and vice versa.

You may decide not share, and that's okay, too. You may decide to stay with the peaceful feeling and allow it to develop into joy. Feel your heart expand as you realize in your core that you are one with all that is. From this feeling joy arises. Let it come; or not as it will. Let love come; or not as it will. Let the peace remain and deepen; or not as it will.

You may decide to interact with your Higher Self during your meditation, which is a wonderful way to bridge prayer and meditation. Try to remember that your Higher Self is really you. You are communing with your Self. Try shifting your perspective and moving from Meditator to Higher Self. They are both you. Leave the Meditator and join with your Higher Self. Feel the peace that exists in your Higher Self. Look out from the eyes of your Higher Self. Does the world look different? Does it feel different? Relax and bask in the "body" of your Higher Self and soak up the feelings so you can bring them with you into the world and have them near all the time.

Don't put any conditions or expectations on your meditation. Just go through the exercise of deep relaxation and reach for the feeling of peace. If it doesn't happen right away, that's okay. It will happen as you practice, and when it does you will enjoy it then. Until that time, be content with the relaxation you have achieved and make a plan to do it again.

Over time your meditations will become something that you look forward to and cherish. You will find the peace you seek. It will lead to joy and love in its own time as you change your mind about your eternal reality and embrace your Self as the one Child of God. You will know that this is the only reality that matters as the hollow feeling you tried to fill with outside things needs those things no more. It is already filled with an inner awareness of who you really are, and nothing outside can ever affect that for long.

Although your time in meditation and active prayer will end and you will get up and return to the world you made, you will find that your inner reality will begin to assume a place in your daily awareness and you will notice that things don't bother you as they once did. You become content to allow events or relationships to develop without trying to control too much. This will feel good, and you will enjoy it, as you should.

> He who has ears to hear, let him hear. When the Blessed One had said this, He greeted them all, saying, "Peace be with you. Receive my peace unto yourself."
>
> —The Gospel According to Mary Magdalene

Meditation takes practice. Although we have the capacity to connect with our Greater Self we have lost the ability to do it naturally. In order to recover this ability we need only set aside time and work through our ego's resistance to an activity (meditation) that will lead us toward our true nature. The results of daily or at least weekly practice will be noticeable, first to yourself and then to others around you who will want to share the benefits you have discovered.

Below are additional meditative techniques. Try them if they appeal to you, not once, but many times, perhaps daily over the course of a month, until you are firmly in control of the material.

Our first example comes from Lawrence LeShan from his book, *How to Meditate, A Guide to Self-Discovery.*

Breath Counting

Counting your breath is a meditation essentially designed to teach and practice the ability to do one thing at a time. It seems simple on the face of it, but do not let its apparent simplicity fool you. It is very hard, requires a great deal of practice, and—if worked at consistently—has definite positive psychological and physiological effects.

Here, however, I suggest that you just try it for fifteen minutes in order to get a sense of what this work feels like. You start by placing yourself in a comfortable position so that you will get as few distracting signals from your body as possible. This may be either sitting, lying on the floor, or standing, depending on your particular wishes. Set an alarm or timer for fifteen minutes, or if this is not available, place a clock face where you can see it without moving your head. If you use an alarm clock or timer, use one with a gentle sound or muffle it with a pillow.

Now simply count silently each time you take a breath out. Count "one" for the first breath, "two" for the second, "three" for the third, "four" for the fourth, and then start with one again. Keep repeating this procedure until the fifteen minutes are up.

The goal is to be doing simply that and nothing more. If other thoughts come in (and they will), simply accept the fact that you are straying from the instructions and bring yourself gently and firmly back to the counting. No matter what other thoughts, feelings or perceptions come during the fifteen minutes, your task is simply to keep counting your breaths, so keep trying to be doing only that. Doing or being conscious of anything else during this period is wandering away from the task.

Do not expect to do well at it, to be able to succeed for more than a couple of seconds at a time in being aware only of your counting. That takes long practice. Simply do your best.

Now begin!

The road of meditation is not an easy one. The first shock of surprise comes when we realize how undisciplined our mind really is; how it refuses to do the bidding of our will. After fifteen minutes of attempting only to count our breaths and not be thinking of anything else, we realize that if our bodies were half as unresponsive to our will as our minds are, we would never get across the street alive. We find ourselves thinking of all sorts of other things rather than the simple thing we have just decided to think about. Saint Theresa of Avila once described the human mind as an "unbroken horse that would go anywhere except where you wanted it to."

Plato also wrote of this problem. He likened the human mind to a ship on which the sailors had mutinied and locked the Captain and the Navigator below in the cabin. The sailors believe themselves to be perfectly free and steer the ship as they feel like at each moment. First one sailor steers for a while, then another, and the ship travels in erratic and random directions since the sailors can neither agree on a goal nor navigate the ship toward it if they could agree. The task of a human being, writes Plato, is to quell the mutiny, to release the Captain and the Navigator so that there can be the freedom to choose a goal and to steer (work) consistently and coherently toward its attainment. Only in this situation when one is free of the tyranny of the whim of the moment can there be real freedom.

A curiously similar analogy is found in the Bhagavad-Gita, a long poem with much attention to meditation and mysticism written in India between the second and fifth centuries BC:

The wind turns a ship
From its course upon the waters:

The wandering winds of the senses
Cast man's mind adrift
And turn his better judgment from its courses.
When a man can still his senses
I call him illuminated.

Our second meditation example is the beautiful "Meditation on God's Light," from Paramahansa Yogananda.

Look at a light and close your eyes. Forget the darkness around you and watch the bright red color within your eyelids. Look intently into that violet-red color. Meditate on it and imagine that it is becoming bigger and bigger. Behold around you a dimly shining sea of violet light. You are a wave of light, a ripple of peace floating on the surface of the sea.

Now watch carefully. You, the little wave, are tossing on an ocean of light. Your tiny life is a part of the all pervading Life. As your meditation deepens, you, a little shallow wave of peace, are becoming the deep, wide ocean of peace.

Meditate on the thought, "I am a wave of peace." Feel the vastness just beneath your consciousness. The wave should feel the sustaining life of the vast ocean beneath it.

Here is another one. It is entitled "Wake-Up Call," and it comes from Stephan Bodian from his book, *Wake Up Now*.

What Are You Really Seeking?

Set aside ten to fifteen minutes for this exploration. Begin by sitting comfortably for a few minutes with your eyes closed. Now ask yourself the following questions: "What am I looking for? What's the goal of my search? How would I know if I found it? How would my life be different? What do I imagine enlightened people have that I don't?" Take some time to reflect on these questions. Be honest with yourself and don't hold anything back. Perhaps you're looking for a quality of silent presence or nonjudgmental openness. Perhaps it's a peace and joy that's prior to the mind and can't be disturbed by thoughts or emotions.

Now reflect on the teachings of the sages who say that what you are looking for is what you already are, that it's not something you need to cultivate or find; it's your natural state, and you've never been apart from it even for an instant. Right now, let go of your search and abide as awareness or presence itself.

Don't try to figure out what this means or meditate in your accustomed way. Just trust that you merely need to let go and be. Rest in the peace and joy of your essential nature. Gaze out at the world through the eyes of unconditional, nonjudgmental presence. The silent presence is what's looking through these eyes right now, and nothing the mind says can make it otherwise. Even concepts like "peace" and "joy," "unconditional" and "nonjudgmental" are superfluous and misleading. Just be who you are!

Continue to remain as you are as you get up and go about your day.

There are many kinds of meditation, and the examples above are illustrations. Meditation is a powerful technique that changes over time on its own. It is helpful to learn different techniques, like loving-kindness from ancient Buddhism, and try them. Another beneficial meditation is the "I am." This is a silent meditation with no thought or action. The practitioner merely inhales as they think "I" and exhales as they think "am." Tantra also has many different meditation techniques that bear exploration. Ultimately "sitting in silence" is the highest form of the art. It is not active. It is a union—the union of your Self with all that is.

When you open your eyes and "return" from time in a meditative state you should not jump up immediately and move to the next task. Immediately after opening your eyes and for at least the next five minutes you will still be in a state of "attunement" with your Greater Self. Relax and enjoy this effect. Allow your mind to gradually return to thoughts of the day, your schedule and plans, hopes and dreams, obligations and concerns.

The Attunement Notebook

You might want to start an Attunement Notebook. This is just pad of paper that you write in after meditating, during that five minutes, while you are still attuned to your Self. Write questions that you have for yourself in the notebook when they occur to you during the day. Questions like: Why did such and such a thing happen to me? What lesson am I trying to teach myself in my difficulties with so and so? What is my purpose in life? How can I best learn love for myself and others? What is the right way to help so and so realize that they are hurting themselves with their behavior? What should I do to let go of my anger about _______? Should I change careers and pursue my interest in X? What can I do in my relationship with so and so to lessen the effect of the ego and grow? If I retire to XYZ location, will it help me to advance spiritually? You get the idea.

Try to stay away from ego questions like: Does so and so love me? or Should I invest in ABC Company? Unless the questions come from a sincere desire to help others unconditionally and grow spiritually, the answers will serve the ego and not your higher purpose.

To use this technique, read the question you want to answer before you begin meditating. Then do your meditation as usual and do *not* think about the question. If it pops up, move it away as you would any other stray thought. After you open your eyes pick up the notebook, read the question and write what you "know" to be the truth from your heart of hearts. The answer may seem very un-profound as you write it, but write it out anyway. Then close the notebook and get on with your day.

You might also want to use the notebook to capture an event that happened during the meditation or a profound realization that you had. Meditations are similar to dreams, and you will find that you retain little memory of what "happened" in your meditation after it ends. It is not necessary to document every twinge of peace or love that you feel. There will be some meditations however, that differ markedly from all the others. Maybe you felt the presence of a loving being who revealed themselves to you and caused something to happen. Or maybe the activity that you were engaged in with your Higher Self took on a life of its own and something completely unexpected happened.

In one particularly memorable meditation, I was in the Temple of Peace with my teachers when I unexpectedly began to vomit nails and tacks and other sharp metal objects while they held me. In another, I was intending to visit a place I frequent in my inner world when my guides took me to a different place where I was told in no uncertain terms that it was not necessary to place conditions in front of my goal of waking to my true reality. Other meditations have had unexpected visitors from my life, and still others have had visits from unknown spirits who laughed and showed me things. These unexpected little voyages within the meditative experience do not fade from memory like a dream. They are retained for years if not the rest of your life. They are not meditations they are visions. They are surprising and beautiful, and they always come with a deep sense of being connected to a reality that cannot be perceived with the daily mind.

In my personal experience these are rare events, and there is no way to predict or encourage them. They are memorable however and are quickly jotted down along with my best guess about their meaning even if it seems obvious.

When you read your Attunement Notebook, don't be surprised if you have no memory of writing the messages in it. You are still very much "in" the meditation during this activity even if it feels like you have come out of it. The thoughts you are capturing fade as fast as dreams, even though you wrote them down. You may also be surprised by the wisdom of your own analysis and advice.

In the end meditation is just a vehicle to help you tune in to yourself for purposes of growing toward and embracing your immortal reality as one Child of God. It should not be thought of as anything more than that. To make it an end in itself is to remove the value it brings to the classroom of life. The feelings of peace and joy and love that you find within can be carried into the world and employed, along with compassion and forgiveness, to surmount the ego's next trap.

There is much that has been written and is being practiced on the subject of meditation. Your heart will lead you to the one that is right for you, and it will evolve to a point where it continues after the formal meditation period is over. After you begin practicing meditation you may find that you are naturally slipping into the meditative state throughout the day. This is a wonderful development and is very beneficial for spiritual growth.

Chapter 16

Love

> *Love is one. It has no separate parts and no degrees; no kinds nor levels, no divergencies and no distractions. It is like itself, unchanged throughout. It never alters with a person or a circumstance. It is the Heart of God, and also of His Son.*
>
> —*A Course in Miracles* W.127.1:3–7

As you meditate and find peace, which is waiting so closely just behind your eyelids, and you dive deeper to allow it to become joy (first in the discovery that you can access your Self and later as you realize that you truly are more than just a body), your joy might begin to deepen into a feeling of bliss as you move into uncharted waters. You are moving into the realm of Love. You might not recognize it. Confusion reigns as we try to make our societal understanding of love fill the void created by our lack of connection to true Love.

True Love (with a capital L) is not the feeling that the movies and storybooks glorify, which is the same feeling that makes your heart leap when someone special walks into the room. Nor is Love the feeling parents have for their child. These feelings exist, of course, and can provoke strong emotions. One need only read the newspaper for accounts of grandiose gestures or even violence that were perpetrated for "love."

That strong emotional and physical response that lovers feel toward each other has been romanticized by poets, song writers and authors, dreamed about, fought over and sought after by mortal men and women since time immemorial. It has also been analyzed by science to reveal the chemical reasons behind it and studied in relation to our instinct to propagate the species. It might more accurately be termed lust. We all know that "happily ever after" mostly happens on the big screen, and we call it a "fairytale" ending. Even though we know "true love" rarely happens in "real life," we want it anyway. We'll have to wait until the chapter on Relationships to learn how to come close to it here in the world, but for now let's discuss Love in the context of our understanding so far.

We are one Child of God who is having an experience called life in which we have forgotten who we really are and lost touch with how to remember our true identity. We also have an ego that has a vested interest in making sure that we don't ever figure it out.

Could it be that our ego is using the strong emotion that we call love as yet another attempt to confuse us and make us think the outside world is real? Could there be just enough selflessness, like that love of a parent for their child, that we could be led to believe true love is possible here in the world? Don't we know in our heart of hearts that the feeling we call love is fleeting, yet we are afraid to admit it because we want it so desperately? If we admitted that, we might have to give up our dreams, too.

"To sleep, perchance to dream—ay, there's the rub." How appropriate if we turn it around. Rather than have sleep apply to death as Hamlet intones, let's presume it applies to life. We are asleep and dreaming. We're dreaming that we're separate from our Creator, and there's the rub! Nothing we do in the separated state will ever cause us to be truly fulfilled and whole. We aren't separate and we have never been separate from God. We just think we are in this dream. That's why the world is forever letting us down. Our belief that we are separate from our Creator is the cause of all sickness and suffering. It is the reason for our misplaced guilt. And that's why "love" as we understand it is so transitory. We are asking it to perform a duty that it can never accomplish.

True Love is the feeling that comes with the complete internalization of the fact that we are not separate from God and are truly one with our Creator and all that is. Atonement is when we realize in our deepest core that we are everything, including God. When we *know* this fact both consciously and subconsciously, we can see our home and we know that it is Love.

Returning to Love is the ultimate goal of our existence. The Holy Spirit's classroom of forgiveness lessons that lead to Atonement ultimately arrives at one final destination, Love. Love is what we are, because Love is what God is. It cannot be defined any further. True Love is not something we are likely to experience while we are also able to perceive ourselves as bodies, for to catch more than a glimpse or a trace is beyond our ability and is not our purpose. "Your task is not to seek for love, but merely to seek and find all of the barriers within yourself that you have built against it" (*A Course in Miracles* T.16.IV.6:1). We do this by asking for help to see our world as a mirror that can aim us toward those areas that need release and by practicing our forgiveness lessons. In this way we remove those barriers and open up to a magnificent energy that is actually our true inheritance.

Love is the God Force, and it is too powerful for this plane of existence. It *is* God, and our understanding is not capable of grasping it. This is as it must be. We will return to Love because we never left, but not while we think we are living on planet earth.

We sense Love, however. We can feel it, thanks to love. But if we could truly understand Love, we would not be here learning lessons in the classroom of form. Just to see it in the distance, however, can produce such bliss that it can alter our life and transform our soul. We long for Love because we believe we are separate from it. We have lost touch with our connection to God (Love), so we use substitutes like love to try and to regain our unity. We have redefined love in our world to mean something that exists between romantic partners or parent and child or close friends. Although those can be noble feelings, they are inadequate substitutes and they do not fill us as we long to be filled.

The ego's concept of love and the true meaning of Love are so enormously different that they could almost be homonyms. The confusion lies in the *feeling* because that wonderful, euphoric, heady feeling we call love is related to the real thing. That is the reason why we seek it so relentlessly; we are actually seeking Love! There are vast differences in depth and longevity between the two, however. One is eternal and profound; the other is temporary and superficial by comparison. It's like trying to understand the ocean when your only frame of reference is a puddle.

This does not mean that we give up on having a "love relationship" or stop loving our family or friends. Far from it. Affection, warmth and caring are all aspects of love and thus of Love. The more we embrace and practice selfless love the more we reinforce our connection with each other as one. We may not be able to fully internalize true Love in this dream, but we can embrace its cousin for what it is: a very strong feeling of connectedness that points the way toward our eternal reality.

Even if it is a shadow of the real thing, love has great power in the dream. Due to its connection to Love, it is a transformational force. Embracing unconditional love for all things and for all the people to whom we are close and everyone we do not know can significantly change the direction of our life. Purity of thought is paramount for transformation to happen. Love with no strings, love with no needs, love for the pure and simple beauty of its essence is all that we need practice. When the feeling arises, as it does quite frequently, because we are beings of Love, notice how it feels and hold it close in your heart. Keep it always nearby and be ready to find it, especially when difficulties arise. In this way we allow love to transform ourselves and our world.

Examples of pure unconditional love are not so hard to find. One need look no further than the family dog. As the old joke goes, if you want to find out who loves you more, your spouse or your dog, lock them both in the trunk of your car for an hour. When you open it, which one is glad to see you?

We laugh because we know that the dog truly embodies selfless love while we must still work toward it. The dog's (presumed) lack of comprehension is no reason to dismiss their genuine feelings. They are a wonderful example of an emotion we may have lost touch with, and in their daily demonstration of it, they can help us all remember what unconditional love looks like.

Love for yourself is also important. So many times we can love other people and the beauty of nature or even the opportunity a difficulty presents, but we neglect to love ourselves. Our dog again provides an example of how we must feel about ourselves. They love us whether we are rich or poor, happy or sad. Even if we get angry at them, they respond with love. If we neglect them, their love is not diminished. The ability to forgive and forget and respond with affection is their primary response to relationship difficulties. Dogs love us for no other reason than the pure and simple spirit that resides within. If they can feel that way about us, surely we can allow ourselves the same opportunity, and love ourselves for the same reason.

Love can transform our small self into the larger manifestation of Self. It is love's greatest purpose. In reality, there are no others and there is no world. There is only one, and there is only Love. We can use the examples that are presented to us to learn to embrace love for others and ourselves as we slowly remove the conditions we have placed in front of it with compassion and forgiveness. Everyone *is* us. When we know this, our hearts will open naturally to everyone we encounter.

We all know that love cannot be "bought." It cannot be negotiated for, and there is no behavior that will maintain the flow of love from one person to another. Many people say that they are "looking" for love and hoping to "find it." They want to meet someone who will give them the love they need to feel good. They tell themselves that they are willing to respond with love if only they meet the right person. The right person will be someone who ___________ (you fill in the blank).

These are ego thoughts, and they will not produce the desired results. The "love" that is described is conditional and dependent. People do not realize that they are indeed negotiating for love. They want to receive the wonderful benefits that come from feeling "loved." The benefit to the person, of love that has been "found" in this manner, is simply a temporary reprieve from feeling undeserving of love in the first place. They tell themselves that they must be lovable because so-and-so now loves them. The ego also has a clear picture of what this love needs to be like and look like and feel like to be "real" and continue to provide those benefits.

Every ego has a different set of criteria. For some it might be affection and attention. For others it may be material goods. Gifts of service may satisfy other egos, while physical companionship and touch may lead other egos to feel loved. As is true of all things ego, this "love" is conditional and predicated on an outside events. It is always shifting, like the mood that spawned it, thus making it infinitely difficult to satisfy. It is not love at all, but attack. It is an attack on one's self through the vehicle of another person and it causes pain.

This is what the ego wants. It wants to create a lifelong search that never ends in success but has just enough good feelings to convince the seeker that they are on the right path. This keeps them looking for love and trying to find it.

In the same way that love cannot be bought or bargained for, it cannot be found either. Love, dear readers, can only be given. What a beautiful turn of events this represents. How simple and perfect it is. In fact, we already knew it! Yet for some reason we forgot.

Now we can embrace love in the only way that gives us, not our egos, control over the process. Now we can allow love to work its magic on ourselves. Now we can employ love the way it was always meant to be used, to make others feel good.

All we need do is remember our friend the dog and give love to everyone in the same unconditional way our dog gives it to us. Maybe it is a smile or a kind deed, or a generous act with no reward expected or desired. Maybe love is given when our partner angers us and thus helps heal the wounds the ego caused. Compassion is an act of giving love that neutralizes bad feelings. In this way we manage love. We use it and extend it. We wield it and project it, and we do it all with the simple act of giving it away.

To whom are we giving our love? To ourselves of course. Love, once given, returns magnified and fills the space inside our heart that craves it. Once given, love returns to beget joy, and in the smiles and the laughter joy creates, we find love. Love returns to vanquish doubt and despair, relieve anxiety and create true hope and confidence born of certainty that the love we give will fulfill its holy mission and return to us expanded, empowered, strengthened, and reinforced.

Love given unconditionally is a true expression of the divine within all of us, and is yet another step along the path to awakening to our immortal Self.

As we give love in our relationships and they respond by moving toward holy, they develop the power to blend two into one. They open us and make the next step into oneness-with-all natural and beautiful.

> In our experience we can say that only love is something which goes beyond duality. When two persons are in love, the deeper they move into it, the less and less they are two, the more and more they become one. And a point comes and a peak is reached when only apparently they are two. Inwardly they are one; the duality is transcended.
>
> —Osho, *Book of Secrets*

We reach for true Love where we find peace and joy as we practice forgiveness. Our job is to remove the barriers we have placed between ourselves and Love (our belief that the world is *not* a dream) by reaching for Atonement. As these clouds part, Love's light will shine on us because it has always been there; it was just obscured. We will feel it, and it is our reward for successfully changing our mind. Love is not of this world, but it is of our Selves. Just being open to that fact will help us achieve our purpose and bring us closer to our eternal reality as One Being of Love.

> God is but Love, and therefore so am I.
>
> —*A Course in Miracles* W-R.V.10:8

Chapter 17

Giving and Receiving

People everywhere, in their quest for happiness outside themselves, discover in the end that they've been seeking it in an empty cornucopia, and sucking feverishly at the rim of a crystal glass into which was never poured the wine of joy.

—Paramhansa Yogananda

Giving and receiving are misunderstood in our world. We give and receive gifts certainly. We engage in a frenzy of it every December whether or not we subscribe to Christian teachings. We give and receive birthday gifts; we give to charity. Some even set up foundations or give extravagantly to institutions. Our government gives money and aid and assistance. We give our time. We may even dedicate (give) our life to a cause or donate a bodily organ.

In every case we are "giving to get." Whether it is known or unknown, subtle or obvious, giving in the world of form is conditional. We all know that the "joy is in the giving" and we do it without any remorse or second thoughts. We have also been taught "give and you shall receive." However, when we give anything of the ego's world we perceive that we no longer have it. We have given it away to someone else and they are the recipient of our "gift." Now they have it, or the benefit of it.

In return for our gift we expect something in return. Sometimes this is explicit. We give our time to our job, and they give us money. We *exchange* gifts at the holidays. Other times our reward is the admiration of others. We'll work very hard to accomplish this one.

Sometimes our selfish motivations are subtle, as when we give ourselves to another person and expect them to give themselves to us in return. Relief from guilt is another reward we expect when we give. Sometimes this is known to us, other times it is hidden as we convince ourselves that our motives are pure.

We keep the running tally going in our mind. If we perceive that we have given more than we have received we feel good. If we have received more than we have given we feel obligated to repay until the accounts are balanced. If we cannot repay we will punish ourselves subconsciously in a misguided attempt to make up our "debt."

This is the ego at work. This is the illusion made real. This is the outer condition infiltrating our inner world for no other reason than to make us forget that we are really the Son or Daughter of God having a dream.

You receive what you give but not necessarily in a material way. You receive what you project from your core. You receive the attitude that you give to others as they (and your world) mirror it back to you. If you give joy to others, you will receive joy. If you give love, you will receive love. We already know this. It isn't necessary to notice when it returns. You become more joyful and loving inside yourself simply by virtue of giving those gifts to others.

Joy, gratitude, love, a smile or a compliment can be given with no feeling of loss or sense that another now has the benefit of them at the expense of the giver. Indeed they grow only by being given freely with no desire that they be returned. That desire for a return will render them vacant and devoid of meaning.

The phrase "virtue is its own reward" indicates that we not only understand this concept, we know that its opposite is the norm. Concepts like "pay it forward" and "random acts of kindness" indicate that we can easily embrace these ideas and they delight our Higher Self. We don't need to receive anything to feel good about giving these attitudes or actions away. They truly are their own reward, and the fact that they don't cost anything is an added benefit.

Positive attitudes return to us a thousand fold. They encourage community and reduce stress in ourselves and others. They move us closer to our reality as one with all, and in themselves are a forgiveness lesson applied. They are the best thing one could give.

The phrase "as you sow so shall you reap" is another indication that we have a common understanding of the concept, but this expression comes with an implicit warning. If you project negative feelings, you will be growing a crop of resentment that will also reflect back to you. As was well said by Carrie Fisher, "Resentment is like drinking poison and waiting for the other person to die."

Blaming others for anything that causes us distress doesn't make us feel better and can actually magnify the distress. Having expectations that result in anxiety if they are not met or happiness if they are is of the ego because it assumes the dream is real. This doesn't mean that we don't expect others to do what they say or behave as we anticipate or that we should not have high expectations for ourselves or others in our lives. It means that our *internal* reaction to failure or success should not be contingent on either outcome. Permitting others to move along their path with faith that the outcome is always for the best because it will bring us all closer to our eternal reality will allow you to accept both defeat and victory in the proper perspective, peacefully.

Jealousy, scorn, shame, guilt, anger, fear, pride, derision, envy, pity, hostility and the like are negative ego emotions that also return to us a thousand fold. We have felt them all before, and we are going to feel them again in our lives. They are opportunities for you! Now you know that you can release them to your Higher Self and let them go! It won't be immediate but it will work better than anything ever has, and this is your proof that the Holy Spirit's lessons of "right-minded" thinking are true.

Negative emotions are also opportunities to resist launching them right back at the "giver" or inflicting them on an innocent bystander in a misguided attempt to feel better. Negative emotions and the actions they cause diminish us and lead us away from God. That's why they feel bad and cause regret, then guilt. These are just some of the ways they return to us. They destroy us inside and have a detrimental effect on the health of our body—which is, of course, another outer mirror of our inner condition.

When someone gives you a negative gift, apply compassion and let it go! Try to see it as one of your own negative thoughts or actions returning to you, and be glad for the chance to release it with forgiveness and ask for inspiration. When you see someone give a negative attitude to another person, respond with a positive gift like empathy but don't buy into their need to retaliate. Realize that all gifts spring from our inner state, and forgive the offender for what they did not do. You might begin to feel horror as you grasp the fact that those negative feelings are coming from a place of self-loathing and the giver is going to have to experience their return. Let it go and realize that you saw it so you could release it in yourself. This will allow you to resist reacting in kind as you are inspired to reply with charitable thoughts for every uncharitable act that you encounter. The phrase, "Don't let it get to you," indicates that we know this in our heart of hearts, but we need to be reminded because we find it difficult to resist the ego's impulsive reactions.

The art of giving and receiving is the concept of karma in its essence. Karma is a universal law. She does not judge but merely operates. Karma of course is of the dream and her purpose is to show us that there is a greater force and a truth we do not see that is very real and is in service for the benefit of all. Karma is a teacher and her lessons may seem harsh, but that is how we learn and move forward at first. We can embrace karma's positive lessons, too, and use them to show others the way forward. Many of us are concerned these days with our "carbon footprint," but in the words of Susan Wisehart, author of *Soul Visioning*, we would do well to remember the effect or our "karmic footprint," too.

It is important to remember that any changes that happen as a result of your greater understanding of the art of giving and receiving are made, by you, in your mind only. They may indeed lead to kindness, words of encouragement and actions of generosity, but they are attitudes that are embodied first and then they may reflect in the dream. As your thoughts about the nature of reality change and you embrace your Higher Self and hold positive feelings in the forefront of your mind, your outer world cannot help but mirror this inner change. You do not need to do anything except change your understanding. All else will follow of its own accord.

Concentrate on giving the gifts of affirmation and empowerment, gratitude, trust, willingness, optimism, encouragement, tolerance, approval and praise, fairness, understanding, generosity, kindness, hope, faith, joy, love, friendliness and respect, because they will kindle a positive flame in your heart and propel you toward God's greater light. These gifts feel good inside and always return to the giver in unexpected ways. They become an upward spiral that lifts your life to the heavens while engendering an attitude of humility, which is the only attitude that can give these gifts truly from the heart with no expectations.

Chapter 18

Sickness and Healing

> *Sickness is a way of demonstrating that you can be hurt. It is witness to your frailty, your vulnerability, and your extreme need to depend on external guidance. The ego uses this as its best argument for your need for its guidance.*
>
> —*A Course in Miracles*, T-8.VIII.6:1–3

For most, sickness is a condition that requires healing so that they can return to "good" health and get back to their life. As far as our physical bodies are concerned, this is true. Many of the common maladies of the human condition have been "cured," and the lifespan of the average person is now as high as it has ever been. In fact, the fastest growing segment of the population is those who are over 100 years old!

A person whose body is physically sick is at a perceived disadvantage to the rest of the population who enjoy good health. They might be considered a drain on our resources, but this is not always the case. Dr. Stephen Hawking is probably the most well-known example of a person who has not only survived but succeeded against incredible physical hardship. Beethoven composed some of his greatest masterpieces after he had gone deaf, and our collective memory is filled with examples of the indomitable spirit of those who faced disease and inevitable early death like Lou Gehrig and Randy Pausch. Their stories encourage us to ponder how they managed to rise to such an occasion and remain strong and inspiring in the face of such an "unfair" sentence.

The proximity of the imminent demise of our body appears to bring forth a powerful ability to heal our soul, and the "curse" of affliction can actually bring out heretofore unknown capabilities if we let it. Certainly some crumble under the news of a mortal diagnosis and shrivel up and die with nary a fight, but others actually rise to the opportunity through sheer force of will and triumph over their adversity. Think of Lance Armstrong. There are so many other examples of normal people who have risen to extraordinary levels due to hardships that would seemingly destroy the average person that whole books have been written about them! While they are still *in* the world they are not *of* it anymore. They have risen above life by virtue of their closeness to death.

These people have reached within themselves and pulled healing out of the jaws of sickness. Many who are healed still die because healing is of the spirit and health is of the body. It is not necessary to achieve physical health to heal as these people have proven. It may be just the opposite. Health prevents healing. Health gives us the chance to forget that our "end" is coming someday, so we don't face our mortality and we do not learn what healing is all about until it is almost too late.

Healing is waking up to your Self. The will to do it is all that is needed. Physical adversity may propel some to find it and that's how we know it is real, but we don't have to experience that level of pain and disappointment to embrace healing right now.

> For the mind that understands that sickness can be nothing but a dream is not deceived by the forms the dream may take.
>
> —*A Course in Miracles* W 140.4:1

Those who have achieved healing realize (if only subconsciously) that the only sickness we need to cure is our fascination with the dream we call life. Once we let that go (forgive it), healing is not only possible, it is certain. It is an internal process. Healing happens in our mind as we surrender to the Atonement Principle that nothing exists outside the mind of God. Good health and poor health are the same thing. They are both sicknesses because they play to the ego's constant pressure to make the illusion real.

> For how can one illusion differ from another but in attributes that have no substance, no reality, no core, and nothing that is truly different? ... We seek to change our minds about the source of sickness, for we seek a cure for all illusions, not another shift among them.
>
> —*A Course in Miracles*, W 140, 7:6, 8:1

Healing cures poor health because it removes its importance and places it where it needs to be: outside our Selves in the illusory world of our dream. We feel peace and love (our natural state), not pain or suffering. We may get well or we may die. It is of little consequence to the healed mind. What are a few more years in the dream compared to embracing our eternal reality?

> Then He continued and said, That is why you become sick and die, for you are deprived of the one who can heal you.
>
> —*The Gospel According to Mary Magdalene*

The fact that good health tends to follow healing is not important. If we are wise, however, we will not wait until circumstances force us to embrace it. We can take the hand of our new guide the Holy Spirit and listen to its counsel with our heart of hearts. We can forgive our companions and ourselves for what we did not do and let the world reflect our release points. We can allow issues to disappear as we give true gifts to others and glow in the radiance of their return. We, too, can be in this world but not of it. We can do it with perfect health and be a quiet inspiration to others who will sense the shift in our perspective and seek to share it with us.

Why wait?

Dear reader, please note, this does *not* mean you will not get sick if you follow the path of healing. It also does not mean that physical ailments will improve, or that you should stop taking prescribed medication even if you start to truly internalize the message. We are not fully actualized at this stage. We are learning a new way of thinking about sickness and healing, that is all. Our bodies will still get sick, we will go to the doctor, and we might have various medical procedures, and that is fine.

We are learning the ultimate truth. In this context, sickness is of the mind, but only in this context. The thoughts you develop will help you place physical sickness and death in a different perspective for your internal consumption only. If you have exhausted all remedies and are near the end of your time here, these thoughts will provide comfort and meaning and hopefully a release from pain. In the meantime, staying healthy while you embrace the truth is the best way to show others that this loving, peace-filled path is one that bears consideration for all.

> When the body ceases to attract you, and when you place no value on it as a means of getting anything, then there will be no interference in communication and your thoughts will be as free as God's. As you let the Holy Spirit teach you how to use the body only for purposes of communication, and renounce its use for separation and attack which the ego sees in it, you will learn you have no need of a body at all. In the holy instant there are no bodies, and you experience only the attraction of God.
>
> —*A Course in Miracles* T-15.IX.7:1-3

Chapter 19

Judgment

Ye judge after the flesh; I judge no man.
—John 8:15

While our mind is healing here the classroom, judgment is the most insidious thought pattern we must overcome. Judgment is one of the root causes of all negative and even many positive emotions. Anxiety, fear, jealousy, anger, pride and hostility certainly trace their cause to a judgment we made, and society supports this kind of thinking at every turn. We make comparisons, which can be judgments, of better or worse. We judge others and even ourselves harshly or favorably. We judge everything from fairness and culpability (in court) to our appearance and sex appeal. We learn this skill very early, and by second grade we are already masters at judging others, ourselves, objects or activities. It is safe to say that no other ego-dominated activity is as deeply ingrained in us as our ability and apparent need to judge. It is a huge driver for behavior.

Our language works against us when it comes to judgment. We say, "This food tastes 'great,'" to indicate that the flavor is pleasing to our palette. "That's too 'bad,'" is how we express empathy. Even the seemingly innocuous reply, "That's good," or "It's all good," makes a judgment and implies that its opposite is lurking just around the corner. Judgments are subtle control mechanisms. We don't even realize how deeply we are invested in them until they are pointed out. The phrase, "civilized" society is a judgment. "Proper" behavior indicates that there is a good or bad, right and wrong way to act. Good luck, bad luck, good weather, bad weather, good girl, bad dog, right way, wrong answer, judge, judge, judge!

Before we go any further, let's make a distinction here between judgment and justice. Judgment is an internal attitude, which we will explore below. Justice on the other hand is a process that is necessary here in the world to promote harmony and maintain our social structure. As a society we are not yet able to police ourselves and crimes are committed every day that must be contained. We have disputes that must be settled, and we have an organization to settle them. We call it the justice system, and we can accept its verdicts without imposing judgment if we want. So, what is judgment and in what ways do we engage in it?

We assign blame to others because we judge them to be at fault. We fear the future because we judge it to be unpredictable. We are suspicious of people because we judge them to have malicious intent. We are anxious because we have judged a future event to portend emotional or physical pain. We are prideful because we judge ourselves to be superior. We are angry because we judged events or individuals to have disturbed our peace. We are jealous because we judged our partner to be untrustworthy. We are hostile because we judge the world to be an intimidating place. We are sad because we judged events and found they did not meet our expectations.

We can also be happy because we have judged that events did meet our expectations. We are optimistic because we judge the world to be a place of fairness. We are generous because we judge our worldly position to be secure. We are kind because we judge that others deserve our help. We are peaceful because we have judged our world to be in order. We are hopeful and have faith because we have judged God to be a good shepherd who watches over His flock.

We judge *everything* from the beauty of a flower to the love of our partner. Then we find it good or bad, wanting or complete, right or wrong. We condemn or accept based on an unconscious set of standards to which we all subscribe. Our collective consciousness even includes a Judgment Day where our lives will be judged by God in the same way that we judge everything in our world!

Judgment is of the ego. Although we will never be able to remove it entirely from our lives, we can make startling progress if we try. It is one of the ego's most effective traps, and it seems so very hard to overcome. "We hold these truths to be self evident…" is a phrase that every American has imbedded in their mind. The implication is that some judgments in the world of form are so obvious that they cannot be argued, and since everyone is in agreement, they must be true. Noble causes top the list of judgments we perceive as good, and torture, pain and death top the opposite list. Nonetheless, these judgments are still ego no matter how "self evident" they seem.

There are certain "judgments" that are necessary, but we don't have to process them as judgments. If we feel fear that someone may harm us, this is an intuition that we should probably heed. Parents must "judge" their children's actions and correct improper behavior and reward pleasing behavior. The boss must "judge" the work of his or her subordinates. If we do this without applying a "good" or "bad" label, we are not judging per se. We are correcting or rewarding or listening to our intuition, and we can do this without passing judgment if we remember that the spark of the Divine is in everyone in equal measure and we are all one.

Judging anything in the world implies that we know best and makes the illusion real. (Is this starting to sound familiar?) It says in effect that we are qualified to decide right from wrong.

We are usurping (our general understanding of) God's place, and that makes our ego very happy.

Judgments do not move us closer to our eternal reality. They keep our attention pinned to the outer world and away from our Higher Self and God. They do not feel good in our heart. They seem necessary in order to cope with our day-to-day reality, but that is not the case. We could simply notice an event or behavior, instead of judging it as good or bad. We could observe and accept. We could feel peace only when it comes from within instead of trying to find it in the world where we have to make a judgment before we can accept it.

You may have noticed that each of the negative and positive judgments listed above was predicated on a condition of the world. That's where judgments come from, the outer world. We have already established that we are the Christ consciousness and the world is an *effect* of our dream. The *cause* is the ego—our belief that we could actually be separate from God. Remove the world from your perception of who you are, and you remove the need to judge it as anything.

You are an immortal, eternal being of light and love. Your true heritage is so magnificent that the entire universe pales in comparison, which is a judgment you would never make if you truly understood this fact.

Unfortunately we do not truly understand our heritage. We can read and study and write and teach for our entire lives and still not internalize more than the basic rudiments of the concept. That's okay. We aren't here to learn that lesson. The purpose of our life is to internalize the certainty that we are the one Child of God having a dream that she is separate from her Source, and that we have an eternal reality that is not part of the outer world that our eyes see and our ears hear and our brains understand.

We are not supposed to *become* the "Son of God" on earth. We are just supposed to understand that we are the Son (or Daughter, or Child, or Christ) and learn to use the world as a classroom to remove all obstacles to truly accepting this fact.

Let's change the above judgments around and see if we can make the positive ones apply to our inner reality. We are happy because we understand that we are so much more than our body or our thoughts or even our soul. We are optimistic because we are moving closer to our Higher Self and we know that will bring good things into our life. We are generous because we know that we receive what we give and we want to share our joy with everyone. We are kind because we know that we are one with all, and as we help another we help everyone including ourselves move closer to God. We are peaceful because we have touched our Awareness (of our ultimate reality) and allowed it to remove our fear. We are hopeful and have faith because we have surrendered control of our daily life to inspiration, it is guiding us, and it feels good.

These attitudes are not conditional on something in the world. If they were, they would be temporary and easily lost. When we judge based on the world, we are closed. When we accept, we are open. The only way we can truly embrace these positive attitudes is if we base them on the eternal, which is never of the world. We accept peace, then our world becomes peaceful. We accept hope, then our world becomes hopeful. We accept optimism, then our world becomes optimistic. We don't have to judge ourselves as a "good person" to accept these attitudes. They are offered freely and are our birthright. They grow through us and extend beyond us. They bring all who encounter them closer to our collective immortal reality.

Most people try to do it the other way around. They judge that if their world could somehow be made happy, they could be happy, too. They try to arrange events to create hope so that those events can then make them hopeful. They reason that if they save enough money, they will find peace. They are asking their outer reality to determine their inner condition, and they have it exactly backward. That's why it never works for long, and they find themselves constantly striving for more.

The ego is the main reason people find it so hard to turn the equation around. The ego is in control and tells us that the world is real and can provide the wonderful feelings we want if only we would just make something happen. It is the ego that believes the world can give us peace and joy and love. Our heart of hearts (and our common sense) tells us differently.

How does one stop making judgments?

Realize first of all that you cannot just stop making judgments. They are far too ingrained. Don't try to change either your need to judge or the effects of these judgments. Acting to change something makes it real. The world is a classroom, and everything that happens to us is a lesson. Judgments call for gentle correction. Accepting this starting point will open you up to noticing your judgments. When you spot one, forgive it immediately by releasing it up to your Higher Self with forgiveness and letting it go.

Start with judgments that produce a strong negative or positive emotional response inside you. You can't miss them. Identify the feeling as originating from a judgment. This is easy because it is almost always the case. Then apply forgiveness and ask for help to release your need to judge. Ask for guidance. If you ask, you will receive it. If you don't ask, it won't come. "Ask and you shall receive" is a law of the universe, and it works in every situation.

Try to notice rather than judge. Things are happening all around you, but you don't have to label them as good or bad or right or wrong. They just are. You aren't in a position to make a judgment anyway, because you don't know if something really is right or bad. If you have trouble overcoming a judgment that seems particularly self-evident, turn it around. Here's an example.

"Terrorists are bad for the world," becomes: "Those who commit terrorist acts are *not* bad for the world." Then think up some reasons why these people are good for the world like, "Terrorists are good for the world because they force us to confront our mortality and in so doing remind us to embrace our eternal reality sooner than we otherwise might." Here's another, "Terrorists are good because they provide the ultimate forgiveness lesson. If I can let go of my judgments of terrorists I can forgive anything."

A compassionate response would be to realize that people who commit acts of terror suffer from a debilitating sense of self-loathing and lack confidence and self-love. Compassion might see terrorists as souls who have been so demoralized by their own pain that they must project it violently on to others.

You can probably come up with a few more ideas or examples if you try, and prove to yourself that you have no business judging terrorists no matter how "terrible" they seem.

This doesn't make their actions "right." Behavior that is harmful to others must not be condoned or supported in any way. We must take steps to protect ourselves from the destructive acts of people who believe they have a right to cause death as we understand that they despise themselves most of all.

Judging them (in our own mind) as "bad people" is the release that needs to happen. We are all one. Every person who has ever lived has the exact same spirit. Some are a lot less in touch with it than others, but we are all equally one Child of God no matter how repugnant some aspects of this Child may seem to us. There are undoubtedly aspects of yourself that you do not like to dwell on for the same reason.

> The Pharisees, in an attempt to discredit Jesus, brought a woman charged with adultery before him. Then they reminded Jesus that adultery was punishable by stoning under Mosaic law and challenged him to judge the woman so that they might then accuse him of disobeying the law. Jesus thought for a moment and then replied, "He that is without sin among you, let him cast the first stone at her." The people crowded around him were so touched by their own consciences that they departed. When Jesus found himself alone with the woman, he asked her who were her accusers. She replied, "No man, lord." Jesus then said, "Neither do I condemn thee: go and sin no more."
>
> —*John 8: 3-12 from, The New Dictionary of Cultural Literacy*, Third Edition. 2002

Jesus doesn't condone the woman's behavior in this story. He forgives her and challenges her not to do it again, thus demonstrating love. He showed the crowd that we are all the same (one) in our lack of ability to achieve a "sinless" life, but never did he judge any those sins as "bad" or "wrong." There is no "right" or "wrong" in the higher spiritual sense. Indeed, his final admonishment respects the spirit within all of us and offers hope that we can all change our thoughts and thus our actions as we embrace the divine and forsake our ego.

It is difficult but not impossible to begin to release your judgmental attitudes. That is what makes success in this endeavor so powerful. It is in fact essential, if you are going to make any real spiritual progress. Luckily, the effects on your inner world are almost instantaneous. This provides wonderful positive reinforcement and makes you want to continue. It is a relief to stop judging! It removes an entire universe of thoughts and actions.

It frees up your mind for more important considerations. It makes you more accepting and opens your heart.

Try using the word "interesting" instead of the judgmental word you feel inclined to use. When you are presented with a person you might normally label as clumsy, lazy, or ugly or a situation you might assess as unfair, improper, or awful, use the word "interesting" (without any tone of voice) to describe it instead. "That is an *interesting* way she disciplines her children." Now it is an observation not a judgment.

Positive judgments are better because they are affirmative. They are still judgments, however, and can benefit from the same kind of solution. Rather than "judge" the situation as correct, amazing, beneficial, or effective or a person as smart, good looking, nice, or talented, try to just notice and describe facts or how the person or event makes you feel. You can still use the above words, but if they are positive *judgments,* that indicates that the negative judgment is not far away. Just notice these situations and do not invest yourself in the judgment as the reason you like something or someone.

"Beaches are great!" could be "Beaches make me feel so relaxed!" Your language and demeanor does not have to become flat or monotone as you remove judgmental attitudes from your thinking, just the opposite. Judgments close you down and restrict your creativity and ability to receive inspiration. Observations and feelings can be described with so much more color and to a much greater effect when the judgment is not present and directing the process.

In the end you will be happier and more content if you stop placing judgments on everything. This doesn't mean you will become mired in indecision because you are afraid to judge what is the best thing to do. You can have reasons for acting that are not based on good or bad, right or wrong judgments. To say that you do not "enjoy" something is not a judgment. It is just a statement of preference.

If you are unsure about whether you are judging or not, do nothing. Try not to use judgmental words when you think either. It is one thing to learn to keep quiet about our judgments; it is quite a bit more difficult to stop thinking them. Thoughts are infinitely powerful, however, and releasing judgmental thoughts is a very big part of the process. When you spot a judgmental thought, apply forgiveness and let it go. This will naturally reduce the number of judgments that you communicate and a peace-filled disposition will result.

There are no "correct" judgments whether positive or negative. To judge indicates that the temporal world is real and plays to the ego's desires. Everything is, in reality, one perfect Self, and how can one judge that? The judgments that you place, or those that are placed on you, are your projections. They are sent out from you or reflected back to you and are ultimately opportunities to forgive the illusion of the separate self.

The only "right-minded" judgment we can make is that everything is perfect, just the way it is. We are not qualified to take God's place and judge anything from torture to euphoria as good or bad. Everything and everyone is God. If we truly believe this fact, how can we judge the actions or motivations of others as anything but a reflection of the perfection that resides within them? We might be tempted to judge the ego of others and tell ourselves that is all right because the ego is not of God. This twisted logic plays to the ego's hand and makes it real. We need only notice the ego to remove it from consideration. Judging it as anything sets up a conflict we can only lose.

This doesn't mean we shouldn't feel motivated to help other people! Nor does it allow everyone's ego to run wild because it is somehow "perfect." It means, as stated above, that we are not capable of making the good or bad judgment. We are certainly capable of feeling inspired to tend to the sick and feed the hungry. This kind of activity is one of the highest forms of recognition that we are all one and that what we do for others we do for ourselves and vice versa.

If you feel inspired to help the homeless, then you should do it. Don't do it because you judge the government to be at fault for creating the situation in the first place and you feel obligated to "fix" their mistake. There is a world of difference between the two. This is an example of how you can re-train your thoughts so that you act from your right-mind (name of a concept, not a judgment) and not from your ego-mind. It is an illustration of the result of applying the ideas we have been reviewing.

As Mother Teresa said, "I was once asked why I don't participate in anti-war demonstrations. I said that I will never do that, but as soon as you have a pro-peace rally, I'll be there." See the difference?

Most of the concepts in this book have a natural effect of removing judgment. As you practice the art of listening to your heart of hearts, learn to apply compassion, reach for and find peace inside yourself, and realize that the outer world is like a dream compared to your eternal reality as one with all, judging will begin to seem unnecessary and even trivial.

As you release your need to judge people and events, your world will begin to reflect your open and accepting internal attitude. The people in your lives will mirror this to you and thus reinforce it. You will realize that the time you spent judging can be used so much more fruitfully embracing love and spreading joy. You will feel content and the feeling will be deep and it will be real.

What is Good and What is Bad

An Apocryphal Fable

A farmer in India had a very fine horse, but the horse ran away. The farmer's neighbor came to express his sympathy at the farmer's great loss. The old farmer's comment was, "Who knows what is bad and what is good?"

The next day the horse came back bringing a herd of wild horses with him. The neighbor immediately came over to express his joy at the farmer's good fortune. The old farmer again said, "Who knows what is bad and what is good?"

The next day the farmer's son, while riding one of the wild horses, was thrown off and broke his leg. The neighbor came to offer his sympathy. The old farmer once again said only, "Who knows what is bad and what is good?"

The next day the army came to the farm looking for recruits. They could not take the farmer's son because of his broken leg. The neighbor came over to congratulate the old farmer on the good luck that his son would still be with him. But all the old farmer would say was, **"Who knows what is bad and what is good?"**

Chapter 20

Relationships and Overcoming the Ego

> *If in your relationships you experience both "love" and the opposite of love—attack, emotional violence, and so on—then it is likely that you are confusing ego attachment and addictive clinging with love. You cannot love your partner one moment and attack him or her the next. True love has no opposite. If your "love" has an opposite, then it is not love but a strong ego-need for a more complete and deeper sense of self, a need that the other person temporarily meets. It is the ego's substitute for salvation, and for a short time it almost does feel like salvation.*
>
> —Eckhart Tolle, *Practicing the Power of Now*

Relationships are the best reflection we have of our inner condition, and they show us how great an influence the ego is exerting over our lives. It is possible to have a relationship that is empowering, and it is possible to sideline your ego desires. Although peace and acceptance are our spiritual heritage, we are not in touch with those feelings very often when it comes to significant relationships. Relationships in the world are the domain of the ego because they are the best way for it to capture our attention and turn it outward.

> It is in the arena of personal relationships that the illusion of a separate self clings most tenaciously and insidiously. Indeed, there is nothing that derails more spiritual seekers than the grasping at and attaching to personal relationships. The revelation of perfect unity reveals the true impersonality of all relationships.
>
> —Adyashanti

"Special Relationships" are what we experience most often in our lives. Until now we have had little choice because we have not learned any other way. Special Relationships can occur between parents and children, friends, siblings or co-workers, but the most instructive tend to happen between special love partners.

In a Special Relationship, we see others for what they can give to us. Affection, pleasure, love, affirmation, hope or joy are not feelings that can be truly received from another person; they can only be mirrored. This is why most "love" relationships run into problems. That wonderful "special" feeling that we get from another person fades and is not replaced by true contentment. We may redouble our efforts to "give" even more of ourselves in a misguided attempt to "get" what we want from the other person. When they don't behave as we expect, our wonderful feeling of "special love" pendulum swings to revulsion as we find our projected needs going unfulfilled. We suffer anxiety, and blame the other person for failing to reflect an image that is consistent with the one we have deluded ourselves into believing we deserve.

> On this side of the bridge you see the world of separate bodies, seeking to join each other in separate unions and to become one by losing. When two individuals seek to become one, they are trying to decrease their magnitude. Each would deny his power, for the separate union excludes the universe.
>
> —*A Course in Miracles*, T.126.VI.5:2,3,4

This is why we "always hurt the ones we love." We subconsciously value highly the mirror they represent. When the reflection doesn't fit with our expectations, we lash out or abandon the effort and soon the person. Our ego soothes our hurt feelings with fantasies of success with a different lover, job, or friend. We "seek but do not find," and in this way the ego keeps us searching in the outer world. We never stop to consider that others may be a reflection of ourselves. If we did, we might change our perceptions and our expectations. We might learn to forgive and look inside for answers to our external issues. Then the ego would lose some control and that might lead to a decision to stop listening to its falsehoods and move toward our Higher Selves.

> In looking at the special relationship, it is necessary first to realize that it involves a great amount of pain. Anxiety, despair, guilt and attack all enter into it, broken into by periods in which they seem to be gone. All these must be understood for what they are. Whatever form they take, they are always an attack on the self to make the other guilty.
>
> —*A Course in Miracles* T-16.V1:1-4

Moving Beyond the Ego

The ego is not to blame, for the ego is us, too. It is our belief that the dream is real, and we cannot blame it for merely trying to accomplish its purpose even if it does cause pain. Pain is the only way the ego can succeed.

The ego is not our adversary, either, for to give it that position accords it a reality that makes it powerful. This causes us to consider ourselves in a conflict with a concept that is illusory. Compared to our true nature as the Decision Maker, the ego is a mosquito, distracting us with bites that cause us to scratch and may sometimes even carry a disease. Just as we do not afford the mosquito the position of "enemy," we do not award the ego the position of opponent. We recognize the risk to our wellbeing that the ego represents and apply gentle correction. Correction notices but does not judge. Correction acts to change the thoughts that allow the ego to thrive. Correction reminds the self of the Self.

The ego can be thought of as an unruly puppy that has never been disciplined. Until recently we did not even know it was there.

How can one correct what one does not perceive? We thought the ego *was* us. Even without knowledge of the ego, however, we have learned to control our basic instinct of self-preservation at any cost. We can see others as ourselves even if we don't do it very often. As our survival needs are met, we embrace empathy and service to others. We are a generous society of humans and hold kindness and humility in reverence. We can be selfless and act for the greater good. These are "victories" we have achieved over our ego's basest desires, but they still assume the dream is "real" and as such do not truly threaten the ego. This makes our resistance somewhat less with regard to these positive thoughts and actions.

The ego is running ourselves and our lives. Wars are still fought over slights, and "man's inhumanity to man" is on display every day in the newspaper. Very few believe that they are not separate from God and that they have the power to embrace their eternal reality.

This is the opportunity of our era. For the first time in history we have a chance to make a giant leap forward that will result in a greater good for all. It isn't a physical opportunity this time. It is not a change we need to make to our outer world. It is a change that we can make inside ourselves that will *reflect* in our world. It is real change because it is a change of perception about ourselves and our world.

Our ego can be brought under control by a simple application of will. Just like a spoiled child, the ego will resist and act to cause us distress. If we react in kind, we will prolong the process. If we but see all strife and success, hardship and happiness in the proper perspective and do not allow them to affect our inner world for long, they will not. We choose our reactions. We allow our egos to run wild, or we overlook its tirades and we notice but do not react to them anymore.

Success in this endeavor takes patience and practice and time. It takes commitment and faith. It takes forgiveness and release. It takes courage and strength. It takes knowledge. Now that we know about the ego, we can see it for what it is, and we can use its reactions to teach ourselves how to move beyond its worldly focus.

Appreciate the ego for its ability to consistently point to the illusion and act as if the outside world could really affect our inner condition. This causes us to remember that all the world's a mirror, and the reflections and the ego aim us toward our release points. Know and accept that the ego will never stop trying to make the dream real. Know that the Holy Spirit's lessons of forgiveness will allow us to affect true change in our heart as we embrace our eternal reality as the one Child of God, and notice how irrelevant the ego is compared to that.

> In actuality, the ego-self doesn't have to die at all; life doesn't come to an end; existence does not cease; and no horrible, tragic fate is waiting to end life at all. Like the ego itself, the whole story is imaginary. One does not even have to destroy the ego or even work on it. The only simple task to be accomplished is to **let go of the identification with the ego as one's real self!** With this relinquishment of identification, it actually goes right on walking and talking, eating and laughing, and the only difference is that, like the body, it becomes "that" or "this" instead of "me." All that is necessary, then, is to let go of ownership, authorship and the delusion that one invented or created this self and see that it was merely a mistake. That this is a very natural and inevitable mistake is obvious. Everyone makes it, and only a few discover the error and are willing or able to correct it.
>
> —David Hawkins

Chapter 21

Holy Relationships

Inherent within the revelation of perfect unity is the realization that there is no other. The implications of this realization reveal that in order to manifest that unity in the relative world, one must renounce the dream of being a separate self seeking to obtain anything through relationship with another. Indeed, personal relationship appears to happen in the relative world, but in reality, all appearances simply arise as temporary manifestations of a unified whole. In the relative world these appearances are in relationship, but not as separate entities. Rather, they are the play of the one Self projecting itself as apparent entities in relationship to one another.

—Adyashanti

If Special Relationships are the bastion of the ego, Holy Relationships are the province of the Holy Spirit. The ego will always try to make every relationship "special." With a little practice you can see the ego at work, and the Holy Spirit is there to help you release your fear.

Holy Relationships are possible when people realize their eternal reality as one with God and all that is and embrace the fact that all seemingly separate beings are in truth merely aspects of the one Greater Self (at "play" according to Adyashanti above). Their forgiveness lessons take hold, and they are aware of their true nature all the time. They realize that the world and especially their relationships with other people mirror their inner status and relationship with *themselves*. They have released their investment in the self and embraced a far more vast vision of their reality that is all inclusive.

Holy Relationships encompass everyone and are not limited to one special partner. Fear is replaced with a knowing that adversity brings us closer to God as we perceive, with our right mind, that all players and events are, in reality, part of us. Judgments happen, but just like hunger, there is an easy solution that satisfies. Gifts of empowerment and affirmation are given as often as possible because, as one Awareness, every positive attitude is actually given to our Greater Self and thus returns in marvelous and unexpected ways.

Peace reigns in a Holy Relationship because it is the inevitable result of the release of fear. Acceptance is followed by inspiration (guidance) and that helps manage any "difficult" times. Hardships may be encountered, but they don't weigh heavily. Apprehension recedes and faith steps in, allowing ego storms to pass because they are recognized for what they are, merely another attempt to make the dream real. If we see the world and everything in it as our Self, how could we not perceive that all is as it should be?

We can turn our Special Relationships into Holy Relationships. Only one partner is needed to make a relationship holy, but if both partners desire it, so much the better.

> Holy Relationships can endure because they recognize that we are all the same: equal Sons of God. They understand that there is no difference between partners (or indeed all people) so there can be no projection of guilt, dependency on another or expectation of reward. Giving and receiving are recognized as the same because as we give so also do we receive that gift. Our perception shifts to Defenselessness where we perceive attack as a call for love. Holy relationships realize that all errors call for correction not condemnation. True innocence exists as both partners surrender themselves to the Holy Spirit and allow him to guide their thoughts, thus relieving them of the guilt of separation and replacing it with the peace and joy of God.
>
> —Ken Wapnick

How can Special Relationships become Holy?

Embracing the lessons thus far in the book is all that is needed to transform your relationships from exercises in maintaining the illusion into a medium that will achieve your purpose for being.

Special Relationships are the final frontier in overcoming the small self (ego) and achieving your destiny. This is why they seem so difficult to surmount. We can understand in the abstract the frame of mind that is necessary, but the Special Relationship comes with one final mountain to climb: our *emotional* attachment to our special separate self, the ego.

No other aspect of the world of form contains the ability to create such strong emotional reactions. No other area causes us to stop moving forward in our search for Self and lose ground as we fall victim to our feeling-self. How many times has a significant other been able to disturb our peace or create boundless joy with a glance or a comment or an action? Why are there only a precious few who can do this, and what gives them such power?

The reason is simple, and the solution not too difficult. The only reason any other person can disturb your calm or create harmony is that you are still invested in your small self and see it as fundamentally separate from other selves. The one last leap has not yet occurred where you truly see all the world and every person in it as one single Self. Fear is holding you back. Fear of the unknown. Fear that you will cease to exist if you embrace the greater whole. It is the same fear that is causing you to continue to make judgments or give while still expecting to get something in return. It is this fear that makes your forgiveness lessons necessary and so repetitive.

Yet you know the Greater Self is there. You touch it during your meditations and receive from it when you ask for guidance or you are "in the zone." You experience the pleasure of true giving and you are able to let go and release judgment. You understand very clearly that we are all one Awareness having a dream that is separate from God. You know that you are not separate, and you forgive all day long and have found inner peace. You have seen the proof!

You have a calm disposition that is happy from the inside out. Almost all of your world is reflecting your progress and your spiritual growth, except for the person who can bring out your emotional ego. So close and then wham! Anxiety, doubt, frustration, annoyance (even anger), abandonment, jealousy, pride, and other negative emotions rear up with a force that astonishes and annihilates the formerly peace-filled mind. *Why is this necessary? Oh God, please help me!*

Oh, the beauty of this reaction! Oh, the power to move the mind! Oh, the opportunity this represents to go forward and never look back! Oh, the blessing! Now you see what you need to release. Now you know how close you are. Now you break through and say goodbye to the small self who awakened the Self and in so doing opened the door that it sought to shut.

Now you know that an act of will that releases and forgives these strong emotions is all that is necessary to replace your "self" with your Self! You can see it! It is the last hurdle. It is the accomplishment.

Release at this height is of the Holy Spirit, and it is totally internal. The delight that accompanies success is a much stronger emotion than the negative one that was overcome. It is a final surrender and an opening of the heart that turns night into day and heals all sickness. It causes tears of joy as you embrace the emotional reality of your release from the dream. Communicating with the other person isn't appropriate because communication at this level isn't possible.

It wasn't another person who caused you the pain. It was you. It was your egoic belief that the outer world is real and has the ability to affect you. Remember no one has the power to create a strong emotional response in you. Only you have that power. Fear gives it to you and allows the ego to make the illusion real. Other people are you! And you are them. Our collective dream has only one dreamer, us! Every aspect of the dream is an aspect of us. It is the outer manifestation of our one Self.

When this realization becomes your inner attitude, Atonement has been attained.

When we enter into a Special Relationship, we form an emotional attachment with another person. When strife occurs, we feel it intensely. If the relationship produces anxiety, we have choices.

We can truly release the anxiety with help from the Holy Spirit and forgive the other person for what they did not do by realizing that the other is a mirror reflecting our own projections. The relationship can then move forward and will be stronger due to the inner release that will, in time, affect the projection, and thus the reflection the other person mirrors to us.

We could instead decide to remove the emotional attachment or decrease it (so that the anxiety is less painful) by convincing ourselves that we no longer care as much about the other person. In other words we might begin to withdraw our emotional attachment. This frequently happens. It is a self-defense mechanism and the result of not being aware of any other alternative or being unable to embrace the forgiveness necessary. This will have the effect of moving the relationship away from its potential and, unless truly corrected with "release," the relationship will probably result in a split-up as both partners agree that they are not "right" for each other and move on.

The "make up" after a "break up" is not release. Although both partners may have apologized and forgiven the other for their transgressions, they have only let each other temporarily off the hook. They will get caught in the same ego trap the next time an issue arises. When that next anxiety develops, it will be powered by the earlier issue, which was not truly resolved or forgiven in any sense. Forgiveness-to-destroy is never helpful in a Special Relationship. Only true forgiveness will allow the relationship to move forward.

All relationships are mirrors, but Special Relationships are magnifying mirrors. They can be so helpful if we understand this verity. In fact, if we did not understand anything else about human behavior except how the mirror works, we would still be poised to take our relationships to the next level. The result will be trust that needs no test. Where there are still tests with pass or fail grades, it is a sure sign of a Special Relationship that is far from content.

When either partner in a relationship recognizes the possibility of a Holy Relationship and surrenders to the idea that their partner really is a reflection of themselves (because we are all one Self), then the relationship will automatically move toward Holy. If neither partner understands this concept, then the relationship will remain special and degenerate over time. The process can be slowed by being vigilant to the other's needs, but in the end no one can provide another person with the right words and actions at the right time to consistently make them feel good. As we have discussed, true peace, joy and love are internally generated attitudes that *reflect* in your outer world. They may be drawn out but cannot be applied to another in place of their own genuine feelings, at least not for long.

It is important to read between the lines and react with love in unloving situations. It is the rule for achieving contentment. The forgiveness that is applied to accomplish it need not express itself in perfect actions and words because it is perfect in itself. That men and women will test, and pass or fail the other's exam is just the manifestation of their shared belief that they are separate individuals and that their actions in the dream have the power to fill the void that is actually created by separation.

The world is the bastion of the ego, and everything is transitory including our relationships with significant others. True security comes from the Holy Spirit and is not dependent on anything or anybody in the world. A truly spiritual person sees a partner's behavior as the mirror it is and forgives the other for what they did not do, quietly and deeply within themselves. Only this kind of "behavior" will result in changing a Special Relationship into a Holy endeavor that brings joy, contentment and deep love to the participants and everyone else in their world.

Emotional attitudes are the mirror and the key. When people begin to understand the concept of a Holy Relationship, they can recognize their dependency on the other partner for a sense of trust in the relationship. Feelings of anxiety become a mirror pointing to areas of release and lessons that need be learned. Insecurities, resulting from a lack of self love, are the "cause" of the reflection, and the feelings and behaviors they generate are the "effect." Focusing on effects is like treating symptoms.

To "cure" the illness, the disease must be found and treated. Then the symptoms will clear up on their own. Finding peace and joy within one's Self where it is eternal and so much more real because it is not dependent on external conditions or people is like finding the illness, the cause of the symptom. Treatment at the level of cause, with forgiveness or compassion and embracing trust-in-faith and self-love, cannot help but relieve the effect of another person's words or behavior.

If the peace does not come, and a person is unable remove the sense that they cannot trust their partner after releasing the emotional reaction, the frustration and the accompanying anxiety, the Special Relationship may not survive. This is okay. In the end, it is an opportunity to learn and grow. Unless the lesson that is learned is one of true forgiveness however, it is unlikely any new relationship will be much different than the old. The same lesson will be recreated by the ego with another special partner in the hope that "this time will be different."

Tests of the other's love or commitment are a form of attack, and the mirror will always show that they are a call for love. When that love is given freely, the tests fall by the wayside as devoid of meaning as the ego that instigated them. When either partner can see past the ego storm and respond with love, contentment is near. If one partner is in touch with his or her Higher Self and can see the other partner and indeed all people as him- or herself, their glow is impossible to deny and their world can only mirror this projection.

If a Special Relationship does not move naturally or consciously toward Holy, it might achieve détente, but not contentment and certainly not lasting love. Both partners simply learn to live with their inability to truly satisfy the other's needs. When that special feeling of love fades, as it surely will over time, and both people run out of energy and any desire to satisfy the other, they will tend to give into their ego's suggestion that their partner was undeserving of their love in the first place.

This is why marriages break up and animosity develops. It is the classic ego swing from love to hate. Both parties listen to their ego and blame the other. They judge that the answer to feeling better lies with another person, and they "seek but do not find" outside themselves for the internal fulfillment they so desperately want.

Every relationship contains the potential to become Holy, but few achieve their promise. Both partners are in touch with neither their masculine nor feminine essence, much less their Higher Self. They may actually have the poles reversed with the feminine embracing her masculine and becoming a warrior in the world of form and the masculine embracing his feminine and trying to put the love relationship first in his life. As they take on a role that is counter to their (worldly) essence, their ability to embrace their Higher Self fades further afield because they have placed a large (and subconscious) complication in front of it.

Coming into balance with your essence as masculine or feminine and recognizing when you are acting in opposition to it is exceedingly helpful for achieving balance with your instinctive drives and helps in understanding the ego's subtle strategy for keeping your attention in the outer world.

If relationship partners continue to believe that their individual external (ego) behavior (what they say and do) is the single most important determinant of their success, they will miss the turn their relationship could take from Special to Holy. Conscious behavior is important, and until forgiveness is natural, it is a starting point from which we learn to integrate real giving and non-judgmental acceptance.

Compassion

As was mentioned before, compassion can play a pivotal role in reducing stress in a special relationship and turning it toward Holy. Compassion sees past the "issue of the moment" to the cause that is driving it. Compassion sees the call for love in the insecurity that drives the difficult behavior and the "tests" that one partner may impose on the other. Compassion results in understanding, clarity and wisdom. It does not provoke a defensive reaction. It draws love forth naturally and, in itself, can foster contentment. So powerful is compassion that if one simply understood and practiced it, all other relationship skills, including the understanding of masculine and feminine, would be unnecessary.

When compassion is *combined* with forgiveness, we have in our hands everything that is necessary to achieve a Holy Relationship. Compassion does not spring forth naturally in any but the most highly developed individuals, but it can be learned and practiced to such a degree that it becomes a way of life. It can turn around the most "hopeless" relationships and render them content. It can infuse all relationships with love and help to create a life that achieves its promise.

The ego will show less resistance to compassion than to forgiveness or atonement because compassion, in the initial stages, still assumes the dream is real. Compassion can take the natural next step, however, into a feeling of oneness, and this is the beginning of surrender to our eternal reality. Forgiveness understands that life is an illusion, but our ego has such a heavy resistance to this idea that we need compassion to smooth the way. Softly, gently and tenderly does compassion release the destructive emotions that keep us pointed outward. Subtly does compassion render the ego obsolete and open the door to the higher realizations. So mighty is compassion that when the ego realizes what has occurred, it is already too late. To the compassionate person who has tasted the truth, the ego's bitter lies are instantly discarded. Forgiveness accomplishes the same objective, and when used together, the combination produces a relationship that sails calmly through all rough waters.

Compassion would never "test," because a test can be failed. Compassion seeks to elevate and never to subordinate another person. Even the slightest practice of compassion can sidestep destructive emotions and draw love from conflict. Thoughts of compassion result in peace, and in this way do we learn the art. The peace turns rapidly to joy and reinforces itself. The "test" on the other hand, has no peace, with even a passing grade resting on the assurance of future successes for mere satisfaction.

To begin to embrace compassion, it is beneficial to understand that we all have moods. Our moods vacillate between high and low all day long. When we are in a low mood, we feel crabby and out of sorts and we react to anything that disturbs our peace with cloudy, negative emotions. That emotion may be annoyance or anger, jealousy, resentment, suspicion, sadness and even self-pity. Our body feels the swell of these emotions as they are carried through our system on a chemical wave that is caused and can even be increased by the low mood itself, if we allow the negative feelings it generates.

Denying the low mood will not help. Recognizing it as a low mood will help immensely, however. Once recognized, the reason can be sought. Maybe forgetting to eat has caused our mood. Unproductive worry may be another cause. The archetypal "bad day at work" might lead us to feel sorry for ourselves or fearful for our future, which can certainly contribute to a low mood. Physical pain, whether a backache, an illness or a hangover, can cloud our mood and bring it down. Maybe we are just over-tired. Chasing the reason is a good way to separate yourself from the mood and look at it objectively.

Once the low mood is recognized, the reason becomes secondary and is merely a device to begin a "thought shift." Moods originate from thoughts. We experience our thoughts. Since we can change them, we can change our mood. Sometimes we don't want to change our low mood thoughts. We want to have a "pity party." If we recognize that this is what we are doing, we might laugh at ourselves and thus break the spell the low mood has cast upon us. Once we recognize our low mood, we might call a friend who we know won't let us get away with it, or watch a funny program on TV while we wait for the aspirin to make our back feel better. Maybe we go to bed early, knowing that we'll feel better in the morning. We all do things to cope with, and get past, low moods. They are not pleasant, we don't like them, and the sooner they lift, the sooner we will "be ourselves again."

One thing we should *never* do in a low mood is have a discussion about an "issue" or a "problem." When you recognize a low mood, take steps to reduce it, like the suggestions above, and ask the Holy Spirit for help to "forgive" the low mood. Then wait. It will lift. Low moods always lift, it is just a matter of time. And as far as your interactions with others are concerned, it is a matter of time-ing. If someone wants to discuss an issue and you're in a low mood, you could just say, "I'm in a low mood now. Can we talk about this after it lifts?" It might sound like a strange thing to say, but it is by far the best way to steer clear of problems. Problems are only real when you are in a low mood.

Apply compassion to yourself. Look into the low feeling and ask yourself what the cause really is. Is it fear? Fear that you will lose your job and never find another one and go bankrupt and become a dismal failure, spiraling down through drug addiction and alcoholism on your way to homelessness? How realistic is that? Is it fear that your boss is going to criticize you every day for the rest of your career? Are you irrationally worried that your friends are going to laugh at you because your hair color didn't match your expectations? Do you feel disrespected by someone? Did something offend your sensibilities? Why would that happen? It didn't bother you when it happened before. Could it be that you are in a low mood this time and that's the difference?

When you are in a high mood, none of these things matter at all to you. In a high mood, problems have multiple solutions and, even if they seem intractable, they don't bother you very much. When you are in a high mood, you feel good. You are happy and the world reflects your joy. This is the time to discuss any "issues," although they won't feel nearly as weighty and they did just yesterday when you were feeling low. Same problem, different attitude. Make a pact to only discuss points of contention when you and your partner are *both* in a high mood. What a concept.

Don't worry that the problem will "spoil" your great mood. If you are both in a high mood, solutions will just arrive, seemingly of their own accord. High moods attract clarity, which opens your mind to wisdom and creativity. The truth is that problems are in the eye of the beholder. Low eyes see problems. High eyes see love. The only question is through which eyes are you looking at the world?

Compassion can help break the spell of a low mood. Whether it is applied to yourself or another, it will have the same effect: understanding. And how could one have too much of that?

> Compassion is a wonderful warm feeling. To suggest you could have too much of it is like suggesting you could have too much joy or too much health.

When people say, "I was too understanding," they usually mean they used bad judgment because they felt guilty or sorry for the person. They acted that way to relieve those unpleasant feelings. As you know unpleasant feelings distort our thinking and lead us to actions we later regret.

When we feel compassion, we are in a healthy state of mind. We have the wisdom to know how to respond to the troubled person. We clearly see without the distortion of negative emotion. We don't regret our actions.

Compassion is misunderstood and undervalued. Without compassion and understanding, interpersonal friction erodes the good feelings in a relationship. Compassion is our innate interpersonal lubricant. It is a blanket of warm feelings that protects us from the rough edges of personalities. When our heart goes out to another person, these warm feelings automatically fill our minds and hearts. Were we not filled with compassion, we would be bothered by the other person's behavior.

Whenever people exhibit counterproductive behavior you can be sure they are in an insecure state of mind. If they were feeling more secure, they would have the wisdom to avoid those behaviors. When we perceive counterproductive behaviors in others, our response is either resentment or compassion. We feel resentful if we focus on the behavior and how it affects us. We are compassionate if we look beyond the behavior to the troubled state of mind that motivated it. We remember how this state of mind wreaks havoc with our common sense. Our hearts go out to the person.

Compassion also protects us against harsh self-judgment. We gain tolerance of our own imperfections. When we feel compassion we can identify with the humanness of life's predicaments. We are reminded of

> how we all occasionally get lost in our thoughts and lose our perspective. Our feelings of humanity are rejuvenated and our spirits rise. The other person gains hope because our spirits have risen from the contact with him or her.
>
> Thus, your compassion helps the troubled person as much as it protects you. Warm, respectful, hopeful feelings are the best gift you can give to a person in distress. Compassion provides the proper emotional environment for the person to recover his or her sense of security. Compassion always delivers an "I understand" message.
>
> —*The Relationship Handbook*, George S. Pransky, Ph.D., p. 49–50

This is our classroom and these are our lessons. They may sometimes seem unkind, but they are not, for to label them thus gives them a reality they do not truly have. When the student is ready, the master appears. He takes many forms, and his teachings are not always gentle. The master is in no hurry, however. We are given an endless number of opportunities and an eternity to succeed if we need it. The amount of time spent in the dream of the separate self is of little significance. We will all arrive at our destination sooner or later, for indeed "we" never left in the first place. There are thoughts we can embrace along the way, and they will help to change our mind about our true Self. As we shift our inner reality, the outer will follow suit. We will notice one day that our "problems" have been replaced with harmony, and our relationships are contented and full of love that need not judge.

Contentment is a rest stop along the road to a Holy Relationship. It is a calm place of comfort where people realize their eternal reality, their significant partners reflect that knowledge almost all the time, and their mirror starts to shine with peace and joy. This kind of contentment is based on communion with the Greater Self. It manifests in our relationships and deepens as it sheds layers of ego beliefs. Trials have been opportunities successfully released for so long that the process is now second nature. A contented relationship simply becomes Holy in a natural fade that is neither planned nor noticed.

Forgiveness is the path to contentment then lasting love in all our relationships. We *can* embrace our partner and all our brothers and sisters as our Selves. It is not so hard; it just takes faith in our ability to make a decision to stop listening to our ego. We forgive and ask for help, we stop judging as good or bad, we give true gifts of compassionate thoughts, emotions and inspired deeds, and we look in the mirror our partner presents for our release points and our calls to love. We allow the Holy Spirit to gently correct our (subconscious) thinking that we are scared and separate little selves until the day we *know* we are not. When this day comes, all of humanity will join us for we are truly one and our success is theirs and their success is ours, which is, of course, as it should be!

> Someday, after mastering the winds, the waves, the tides and gravity, we shall harness for God the energies of love, and then, for a second time in the history of the world, man will have discovered fire.
>
> —Teilhard de Chardin

Chapter 22

Prosperity, Abundance and Attraction

> *One of the basic lessons of spiritual growth occurs when you realize that you will never be fulfilled for very long or very deeply by anything in life. Even things you work really hard for, when you get them, are just another moment. There are some tremendous moments of happiness in life, but they pass. And even while they last, there is always the tension and fear that they might not last too much longer.*
>
> —David Deida

Maybe you have heard of the Law of Attraction? Maybe you have been drawn to learn "secrets" because you want a more abundant life? Maybe you perceive a lack in your life that needs to be filled, and you are inspired to acquire what you think you need?

Maybe you want the "nicer things" in life? Maybe a wonderful vacation is just what the "doctor" should order for you? Maybe a big house or a new car would make you happy? Maybe a new job, too, and make it one with meaning and significance, if you please, Mr. Universe! Maybe you could even attract a family that doesn't bicker and parents who don't put too much pressure on you?

Maybe money is what you need? Maybe you think about money all the time and really need to attract a lot of it? Maybe now you realize that it isn't about the money? Maybe you remember the tongue-in-cheek humor of Phil Hartman: "It's never about the money. It's about all the things you can *buy* with the money!"

Maybe you want good health and a fabulous relationship with a wonderful partner? Maybe you have been led to believe that all you need to do is to be inspired and events will conspire to bring you your desires in great abundance? Maybe someone told you that the universe is poised to deliver your wildest dreams right to your doorstep, and you believed them?

Maybe you don't understand why it isn't happening to you? Maybe you think that you aren't doing it right? Maybe you are frustrated, and that's the problem? Maybe you just have to overcome frustration with the process and it will work? Maybe you haven't given it enough time? Maybe you don't "get it" after all, and maybe you won't get your dreams either! ☹

The Universal Law of Attraction is certainly in operation. One need only look at one's own life and the lives of friends and family to see it in action. The concept that you are living the life that you manifest is true along with the fact that if you don't like it you can change it.

The thought that wealthy successful people are happy and poor people are miserable is a misconception that most people believe. While there are unhappy poor and destitute people in the world and there are happy affluent ones, this is not always the case. The attraction of material prosperity and abundance does not guarantee happiness. If it did, we would not have drug-addicted movie stars who can't maintain a relationship and Buddhist monks would be depressed. It seems that quite the opposite is true. Truly happy rich, successful people seem to be the exception, and the Dali Lama, a man who has every right to be depressed with the loss of his homeland over forty years ago, finds humor in almost everything and laughs constantly.

Thoughts are the most powerful force in the Universe, but thoughts of material success and the idea that joy can be found in "things" or soul mates is yet another attempt to draw meaning and satisfaction from an ego-based reality. We can manifest physical objects from the world of form if we think about them and desire them and work at it, but what are we really attracting? If the answer lies with a thing or a person or a healthy body, we have fallen, yet again, into the trap the ego has set. We are acting as if the illusion is real and believing it can provide inner satisfaction. It can't. Even Tom Brady, the three-time Super Bowl winning quarterback for the New England Patriots, said, in a *60 Minutes* interview, that he often wonders if "this is all there is."

Those of us who aren't rich and famous think it "must be nice" to be rich and famous, and we fantasize about how happy we would be if we were rich, and maybe we decide to skip the famous part because that seems to be where all the trouble comes from. Those who are wealthy and successful actually feel the same inner sense of lack that the rest of us do, as Tom Brady so conveniently showed us with his question. Their problem is that since they already have the money or the power or the status, they can't lust after it and tell themselves that when they get it, it will bring them fulfillment. They usually find something they still "need" and chase that next, or their ego helps them create a great big and sometimes very public problem that occupies their time and attention.

Most of us don't know what we really want. We move passively through life and accept what it hands us and complain or consent, and we wonder. We wonder, like Tom Brady, if this is all there is? We wonder where the meaning is to be found. Just before mid-life, we start to wonder what we want to be when we grow up. We may even have a crisis as we realize that our dreams may never become reality and the time for them is nearly gone. With the passing of the joy of youth, the regret of the middle years can set in and it might be followed by the resignation of later life. Along the way, we somehow failed to find the things or the people who could make us happy. Instead we wound up with a garage full of stuff and people who irritate us more often than they appreciate us.

We read books telling us that to find happiness we just have to manifest what we desire. But we don't know what we desire, so we decide to desire what everyone tells us we want: more things from the world! Bigger houses and faster cars, perfect love, fun vacations and admiration for our accomplishments. We decide to want that, and we admire people who have those things. We idolize them. We emulate them. We strive and we work tirelessly, denying ourselves time today so we can have those things tomorrow, or worse, we borrow from tomorrow so we can have them today. And the matrix supports our thinking, and the ego is in its glory.

Do we attract our desires? Do we get what we want? Of course we do. The Law of Attraction works like gravity. We bring positive and negative situations, people, events and outcomes into our life. We do it all by ourselves with our thoughts and feelings. Thoughts and feelings really are the most powerful force in the universe. The part most people don't realize is that our *unconscious* thoughts are the influential ones. The thoughts we *don't* know about are the ones that are manifesting all around us. As was pointed out earlier in the book, it takes hard work and mind training to consciously change our unconscious thoughts. Our subconscious is the part of the iceberg that is *under* the water, remember?

If we are having negative conscious thoughts and we make them positive, our life is going to improve almost immediately. This is no secret; it is common sense. Results that appear from this change of attitude are hardly miraculous, they are long overdue. This is the easy part, and if you haven't done it yet you should. Your life will improve so much by comparison that you might be tempted to think you've accomplished the entire objective. Beware however. If your conscious thoughts are negative, your unconscious thoughts are even more so. If you are naturally a pretty happy, buoyant person, you may be tempted to think that your subconscious thoughts are that way, too. Look around you. Examine your satisfaction level with every aspect of your life. This will give you a good idea of what your ego is dwelling on subconsciously.

Changing your subconscious thinking patterns and figuring out what you truly want is the real work. So, what do you want in the deepest core of your heart of hearts?

I would submit that if you were to boil it down to its essence, what you want is to feel true peace and have a calm disposition that cannot be ruffled. You want a happy attitude that springs forth from abundant joy, and you want to feel authentic love all the time. You want your life to be guided by inspiration, you want your work to be meaningful, and you want to see your positive feelings reflected in the face of everyone you meet. Am I right?

This is what we all want and how we go about manifesting it will make the difference between a life that "sought but did not find" and one that achieved its promise. True abundance and prosperity cannot be found in the world of form. Material things can be attracted, and this is mistaken for prosperity. We already have more abundance than we know what to do with. It isn't what we want. Its pleasures are short lived, and they do not satisfy. Indeed they keep us lusting for more. Unless we learn a different way of defining affluence and plenty, we will never attract what we truly desire.

We have this wonderful ability to manifest things in our life. They don't just happen. There is no such thing as coincidence.

We are the Author. If we write the script, we align the forces, and the universe hands over what we ask for, why aren't we happier and more satisfied? Could it be that we are listening to that little devil on our shoulder and buying into the illusion that the outer world can create inner harmony? We have seen so many examples of the power of our intentions to create our external reality. Maybe it is time to use those powerful intentions to affect our inner world.

Most discussions of the subject of the Law of Attraction focus on thoughts and actions that illustrate the answer to the question of *how* and give almost no attention to the question of *why.* Why in the world are things set up this way? Why are we able to attract and manifest in the first place? Why do we seek solace in objects and superficial relationships? Why don't we feel content? Why do we lust for more? It is in the answer to the question of why that the meaning is found. Once we understand the reason, we can seek our heart's desires where they really are and stop searching for them where they are not.

Maybe we have been listening to our ego. Maybe we believed our ego and thought that we were separate little selves competing with others for our fair share. Maybe our world doesn't have to be full of things before we can experience joy. Maybe we desire the wrong things.

Maybe we are not what our ego wants us to think we are. Maybe we aren't our body or our thoughts or even our soul. Maybe we can learn to listen to our heart of hearts. Maybe we are the one Child of God having a dream that we are separate from Him. Maybe that's why we can attract things, and maybe that's why the universe does our bidding. Maybe we just don't realize our true heritage. Maybe we could decide to learn about it and embrace it.

Maybe we can learn to listen to the Holy Spirit. Maybe we can touch our Higher Selves. Maybe we can attract inspiration. Maybe we can release our fears. Maybe we can forgive our brothers and sisters for what they did not do. Maybe we can notice our ego and let it storm past like a bull through a matador's cape.

Maybe we can learn to give with no expectation of reward. Maybe we can stop judging and accept others as our Selves. Maybe we can heal our spirit and never experience sickness.

Maybe we can attract true peace. Maybe love for all things is within our grasp. Maybe our world and the people in it really are a mirror of our inner condition. Maybe we can change our inner reality and watch our external one shift along with it. Maybe we can have a contented, holy relationship with everyone we know.

Maybe the world is a classroom. Maybe we are here to realize one simple truth. Maybe help is only a thought away. Maybe we can attract true abundance and prosperity, and maybe they don't have anything to do with things or people. Maybe we are everyone, and they are us.

Maybe we truly are the Christ consciousness and the world is a manifestation of our one Greater Self. Maybe our true inheritance is so magnificent that we cannot imagine it or describe it or even embrace it while we believe we are in a separate body. Maybe we can wake up to our true reality as the one Child of God and leave our small self (ego) behind as we embrace the Greater Self and suffer nothing but bliss.

Maybe we can actually experience the benefits of this new way of thinking almost immediately. Maybe this will prove to us that there is a better way. Maybe our purpose in the world is to change our mind about the nature of reality and listen to our heart of hearts so we can experience true peace, joy and love. ☺

Universal Laws

The dream is governed. There are laws by which it operates. Some of them are well-known and pertain to our physical reality, like the Four Laws of Thermodynamics or Kepler's Three Laws of Planetary Motion. The Law of Gravity is one with which we are all familiar. We easily grasp and understand these laws even though we cannot perceive them with our five senses. They pertain directly to our world of form, and they do not require our belief. They have always existed and were merely discovered by people and employed to understand and improve our lives. They can be measured and applied and are extremely consistent in their behavior.

There are also universal spiritual laws that affect our lives. These are not as well understood because they seem to be less consistent and do not fit the general scientific definition of a "law." There are over sixty identifiable universal spiritual laws, of which twelve are Master Laws. We have covered a number of them already in the book. As You Sow So Shall You Reap is well-known and covered in the chapter on Giving and Receiving. The common understanding of the Law of Attraction was briefly covered above. It is really the Law of Manifestation that people are seeking to employ with their efforts to "attract" abundance into their lives. The Law of Cause and Effect is the Master Law that contains the Law of Attraction, which actually fits in under the Law of Like Attracts Like, right next to the Law of As You Sow So Shall You Reap. These laws are influenced by the First and Second Laws of Increase. The Cycle of Karma is also a universal law.

Whether we like it or not, these laws affect our lives every day in countless ways that we do not see because we are neither aware of them nor open to them. Our understanding of their functioning is very rudimentary and we are unable to determine which rule is governing any given situation. Just like the law of gravity however the laws do not require our understanding. They operate smoothly and exist to assist with our soul's development. Understanding a little about how they operate is helpful because they always point to the Self. The overwhelming message in the study of these phenomena is that thoughts and attitudes are far more important than deeds and actions.

Purity of thought and intention, with love as the central operating principle, will cause our lives to naturally fall into alignment with these laws. They bring home the lesson that we cannot fool the universe, which is, of course, ourselves. If we harm another, the laws insist that we will be harmed; if we act for selfish gain, we will receive pain instead. If we act from genuine kindness and give love with no expectation, those attitudes will return to us magnified. The laws themselves have no agenda but they are consistent, and as such they help our soul progress in the dream.

Our Higher Self is always trying to help us escape from the illusion of the separate self. Universal laws represent a system that will naturally move us forward along the path out of the dream. The Law of Attraction actually states that we will be "attracted to that which will move us forward." The Law of Repulsion states that we will be "repelled by that which will not move us forward." We must take care, however, to understand what these laws can and cannot do.

Universal spiritual laws can keep us trapped in the dream by focusing our attention outward and giving us "proof" that our conduct and attitudes, thoughts and aspirations, deeds and actions have a real effect here in the world. They do have a real effect in the "dream world," and that can be a problem. We have all spent countless lifetimes working on aspects of our soul's journey in our attempt to accomplish the objective, which is to return to the state we never left. More often than not the ego conscripts the laws and points them outward. We start to believe that we can manifest heaven on earth. We can thus lose track of our goal as we slip deeper into the dream, which becomes ever more pleasant.

> The [person] hopes to learn how to get the changes he wants without changing his self-concept to any significant extent. ... The self he sees is his god, and he seeks only to serve it better. ... Resistance is its [the ego's] way of looking at things; its interpretation of progress and growth. These interpretations will be wrong of necessity, because they are delusional. The changes the ego seeks are not really changes. They are but deeper shadows, or perhaps different cloud patterns.
>
> —*A Course In Miracles* P-2.in.3:3,6; I.2:4–7

When we are in alignment with these universal laws, our life improves to such a degree that we believe we have indeed found the true path home. The laws operate with such goodness and wholesome godliness that it is hard to believe they can become one of the ego's most subtle traps if we allow it. In and of themselves, universal laws can do nothing more than make our existence more comfortable in every dimension of duality, and if we understand this, we can move beyond the world they seek to verify.

While we are practicing our forgiveness lessons here in the world, we can use the laws to remove our problems and our anxieties and help us find the peace, joy and resources we need to transcend the laws themselves. Treating others with kindness and purifying our thoughts so that we act without guile is a first step in embracing oneness with everyone and everything. Oneness with all things becomes oneness with God, and embracing this heritage is what waking up from the dream is all about.

Universal laws only exist if there is a universe. Take away the universe, and you remove the laws, too. The "universe" means everything that is separate from Source. *We* are not separate from our Source, we never have been, and no matter how often universal laws prove that the outside world exists (because it can be affected by our inner condition), we will never be separate.

When we wake up to our eternal reality and we realize that we truly are one with God and nothing else (because nothing else exists), we leave the laws and the ego behind and return to the place we never left.

> The world you see is what you gave it, nothing more than that. But though it is no more than that, it is not less. Therefore, to you it is important. It is the witness to your state of mind, the outside picture of an inward condition. As a man thinketh, so does he perceive. Therefore seek not to change the world, but choose to change your mind about the world.
>
> — *Course in Miracles* T.21.in.1:1,8

Chapter 23

Listening to Your Heart of Hearts

We are not human beings
having a spiritual experience.
We are spiritual beings
having a human experience.
—Teilhard de Chardin

Our heart knows the truth because it has always known the truth. We have forgotten how to listen to our essence. It is easy to overlook. It does not demand or insist like the ego; just the opposite. It quietly knows. The knowledge is ours for the taking but we have to re-learn how to ask and how to hear the answer. It is sometimes difficult to tell the difference between a quiet ego thought and a true heart of hearts thought. Ask yourself how you feel in your "heart of hearts" about a particular situation and wait for the answer.

If we can't tell how we feel, we may be blocking the answer because we don't want to "hear" it. We are afraid, and that is what the ego counts on. We imagine all kinds of potential problems. We talk ourselves out of things. Remember the ego never takes a chance on forward progress. The ego has worries and doubts and fears. If our heart is attracted to a new job or a new beau and the "other" half of our mind is worried about all the "what if" situations, we may very well have a classic confrontation between the ego and the Higher Self.

We might also be afraid of admitting a "lack" in ourselves. The ego never wants to admit weakness. Asking for help or accepting love may be seen, by the ego, as admitting a failing. The "quiet voice" may be very open to the help, but it gets drowned out so often by the ego that we don't even perceive it anymore. Check to see if it is there. If it is, allow it to be heard by just considering the possibility.

We should try to recognize these kinds of scenarios as opportunities to embrace our Greater Self. If you are having trouble getting an answer for a question from your heart, ask yourself: what is the "right" thing to do? Not what is the easiest, or the most profitable or the least obtrusive or the safest thing to do. Think about what is the *right* thing to do. Many times the loving thing is also the right thing to do but we have powerful egoic resistance to attitudes that come from the Holy Spirit. Your resistance may be a clue that you are listening to your ego.

Make that "right" decision, in your mind, to go against all those worries and take that job! Agree, in your mind, to accept help from that "ridiculous" source. Try on the decision mentally. Play with the idea. See how it feels in your heart. Does it feel true? Does it feel "right"? Of course there are pros and cons. If there weren't we wouldn't be having a hard time with the decision. After playing with the idea in this way, drop it and wait for something to happen. An event might occur that makes the decision easy. Whatever is decided, this kind of thinking will help us move closer to our source. Source is that to which our heart is connected. The simple act of trying to listen will open the door, and tuning in to our heart of hearts will get easier as we do it more often.

In the end, every situation, and indeed life itself, is an illusion that "we" created so we can grow back to the place we started. The greatest difficulties cause the greatest opportunities for growth. The heart of hearts decision to leave a safe relationship may result in pain. Staying in that relationship should have been easy yet something drove you out and you resisted your ego's advice to play it safe. You took a chance with your heart and now you feel awful. Everything is ruined. "I really blew it," you think, as your ego takes you to task.

What happened here? You took your time making the decision. You listened to your heart. You went against your ego. You did everything right, yet it didn't work out and now you feel terrible. It felt like the right thing! Ask yourself if there wasn't some of the ego in that decision. Were you leaving an unloving relationship for a more loving one that didn't materialize and that's why you feel bad? Were you asking your outer world to provide inner satisfaction—again?

Maybe the idea to leave the relationship came from your heart but you allowed your ego to run headlong into the (perceived) safety of the next relationship. In other words, you chickened out on the real opportunity for growth that leaving a difficult relationship presented. Now that scared, lonely, unloved feeling is, yet again, an opportunity to achieve that growth.

Nothing went wrong. Everything is operating perfectly. You expected that a heart of hearts decision would result in something nice and warm and comfortable right away. You still think that the outside world can create inner harmony. The Author of your life is trying to teach you that it can't. The Author of your life is "you." Your Higher Self wants you to grow spiritually and every so-called "terrible situation" is an opportunity to learn a lesson and grow.

We aren't here to have a nice comfortable life with a minimum number of problems. No one has that! If you think they do, you don't know them very well. Everyone has a Greater Self who is lovingly steering major life issues right into their path. Why does this happen? So we can learn a lesson and grow toward our

Source. That's why we are here in the first place. We are learning lessons in the classroom of form.

The lessons can be hard, just like life. Welcome to the classroom.

Sometimes the choices are both "bad." Stay in the stressful relationship or leave it for an (imagined) life of loneliness and poverty? What to do now? Celebrate! You're going to learn a lesson no matter which one you pick. You're not doomed, you're saved! "You" decided to teach yourself the lesson, right now. No more waiting. If you think back on it, you can see that the tension was building like a flood against a dam. Now the dam has burst and you are staring "opportunity" right in the face; it just doesn't feel like an opportunity.

The change of mind that results in you perceiving every difficulty, and especially every "impossible" life situation, as an opportunity for growth is the thought that will turn the tide and remove the negative feelings from the situation. In the same way that compassion pushes defensive reactions to the side, realizing that difficulties are opportunities, will remove our ego orientation and allow us to "get" the lesson. The simple act realizing that there is a lesson (and this feeling isn't just happening because of the outward event) will separate us from the effects of the lesson and give us that "opportunity." Learning this is, of course, the first lesson.

The ego's lessons will always try to teach us that the outside world is real and has the ability to truly affect our inner state. When we find ourselves feeling angry or anxious or worried, it is an indication that we think events have power over us and we are surrendering to our ego's teachings. When we realize that this is an opportunity to learn and grow, we are embracing the Holy Spirit.

When we embrace the ego and act greedy or behave with our own selfish interests at heart, the universe (our Author) will react to teach us a lesson. It might not be immediate but it will come.

> Therefore, hold no one prisoner. Release instead of bind, for thus are you made free. The way is simple. Every time you feel a stab of anger, realize you hold a sword above your head. And it will fall or be averted as you choose to be condemned or free. Thus does each one who seems to tempt you to be angry represent your savior from the prison house of death. And so you owe him thanks instead of pain.
>
> —A Course in Miracles W-pI.192.9:1-7

A true Higher Self decision might feel scary as soon as we do it, and we might second guess our self, especially if things don't go according to our beautiful plans. The growth that results will soon render this decision one of the best things that ever happened to us, however. The Author of our life loves us. She doesn't want us to suffer. She wants us to learn the lesson and grow. As soon as we do, the pressure will recede. We'll feel it. We will know that the best thing for everyone just happened. A period of peace and joy will result. We will "get" the lesson.

Growth takes many forms and is always tailored to each individual. Learning empathy may be one lesson. Kindness is another. So is generosity and humility. Being honest with yourself is a big one. Gratitude is a wonderful state of mind, and learning it could be the subject of one or more of our lessons. Trust is critical and the subject of many lessons large and small. Faith is another. Learning to give from the heart and employ compassion will turn a gray sky blue. Each one of these lessons is an attribute of our Higher Self. We're here to embrace them, and everything in the dream world is orientated to helping us do just that. This is why every "bad" thing that happens can be thought of as "good."

When we learn a lesson, events turn positive and we can see them, too. When good things happen in our life, and they are accompanied by a peaceful feeling that all is well and we are doing the right thing. This is the outward effect of the inner change. If we notice positive events and are able to connect them to a change of heart (the lesson that we learned), they become powerfully self-reinforcing. Maybe you gave your time unselfishly and were rewarded with a winning lottery ticket. The two events may seem unrelated and we can never tie the causes and effects together precisely. We can realize however, that the change of mind (growth) that accompanied the learning of the lesson will result in positive effects in general, and this is enough to keep us going. "Instant" karma is the same concept, except that the results (either positive or negative) are immediate and we can see how our thoughts and actions play out in the dream.

Lessons never stop. They ebb and flow in our life based on how well or how poorly we embrace the teaching internally. As we discussed earlier, if we don't "get" the lesson, it will return again and again in a different guise. We might not get the lesson in this life. If we don't, we will have more opportunities in our next life. That is why we incarnated in the first place. We have been working on especially important lessons for many lifetimes, and this is merely a continuation of an ongoing activity that will eventually result in our return to the place we never left.

The overarching "lesson" we come to learn is love. Love isn't a lesson in the same way that gratitude and humility are lessons, however. Love is a conviction. Love is one. Love is realizing, if only for an instant, that we are not separate. Love embodies all lessons and is part of them. All lessons lead to love, and that final surrender makes negative lessons unnecessary. Love knows all lessons and need not learn them.

We take baby steps toward Love as we understand that difficulties are opportunities. We begin to learn and grow toward our ultimate reality, one lesson at a time. When we understand what is going on, we make much faster progress. One day love comes to us.

Learning to listen to our heart of hearts, that still, small, sure voice that we all have, is the key. It will tell us, if we ask, whether we are moving in the right direction. True peace will come, and that's how we will know. The Holy Spirit is here to help us recognize our ego responses.

Forgiveness is the best way to remove the fog that clouds your understanding of the fact that all the world's an illusion designed to keep us asleep and away from the knowledge of our true reality. We can move beyond this dream however as we come to understand that we are not separate from Love. When we get this lesson, we become an inspiration to others and our work continues. It is joyful work.

Until this happens, your heart of hearts can guide you and protect you and keep you on the path that brings you home.

Chapter 24

Waking Up

> ...Your life is not a part of anything you see. It stands beyond the body and the world, past every witness for unholiness, within the Holy, holy as Itself. In everyone and everything His Voice would speak to you of nothing but your Self and your Creator, Who is One with Him. So will you see the holy face of Christ in everything, and hear in everything no sound except the echo of God's Voice.
>
> —*A Course in Miracles* W151.12.1–4

We are asleep and dreaming that that we are awake. When you are dreaming as you sleep in your bed, you believe you are awake then, too. When you awaken in the morning, you realize that it was a dream. Waking to our eternal reality is like that. And, it is not like that.

It is the same because we realize that the world is a dream and we are the almighty dreamer, but it is not like a dream because it continues even after we awaken from it. The dream doesn't change, but everything becomes different.

"Spontaneous awakening" with little preparation does occur but it is rare. Suzanne Segal awoke while boarding a bus in Paris and Robert Adams unexpectedly achieved enlightenment in seventh grade math class. A review of the events that led to these experiences reveals that Segal was an avid practitioner of Transcendental Meditation even though she had stopped the practice years earlier and Robert Adams had a psychic relationship with an Actualized Master, Ramana Mahrashi, which dated from his earliest memories in the crib.

All awakening is spontaneous in the sense that it is unexpected, but there are activities and thoughts that we can engage in that will invite the experience and help prepare us for it. Without preparation the occurrence can be misunderstood and quite shocking. Segal for instance spent years trying to shake it off and get back to who she was before it happened.

Adyashanti's awakening experience is instructive. From his earliest memories as a young child, he was aware of a powerful Presence living inside himself, yet he gave no credence to it and spent years in the study of Zen Buddhism trying with all his power to awaken. When he gave up and surrendered to himself, the Presence moved to the front of his awareness and he finally recognized it as the knowing that he had been trying so hard to find. It had always been there and he had always known it.

Even though no two awakenings are the same and the experience is beyond words, it is usually precipitated by feelings of being drawn inexorably toward something significant and profound.

The first stage is to come to believe that there must be more than your eyes see and your brain understands. This is the initial opening to guidance from the Holy Spirit. People and events in the dream will conspire to provide clarity and the door will open wider because you wanted it to open wider, and you will read a book or meet a person or attend a seminar because your sister dragged you there. The door would not exist if you were not ready to walk through it.

Something in you pulls you toward the light and sparks a fire deep within you to continue. Pathways open and lead you in, and it feels good so you learn more and you open more. Then you become afraid and pull away because your life has gone astray and problems that require your attention must be found; and so they are. Later you come back, for you cannot stay gone for long after you have touched your destiny.

Now you begin to learn in earnest. You seek and you strive. You open with all your heart and mind and drive the things you need to your side. And you eat them up. You didn't know that you were hungry, but you were, you find.

And the world assumes less importance as your peace grows strong inside. Your friends ask how you've managed it, and you feel real surprise to see that reflection. You had thought that nothing had changed, and now you understand that your brothers feel what you have found and they want to know it, too, if they can. You smile and you say that you have discovered a different way of seeing the world. And you give them a thought and help them to see that their problems are not the problem.

You have reached the stage where you know that "you" are running the show called life. You know your ego, too, and your belief in its whispered worries fades until it has to cause a crisis. And when you take it seriously and act on its demands, you see the error immediately and wonder why you fell from your own grace. Then you see the reason was to teach you to reach beyond the lessons that you thought you were learning.

You begin to be in the world but not of it. Your life goes on with joys and heartache, but you are smooth and calm inside. You partake of worldly goals, but their achievement seems strangely thin. Tragedy and horror, too, weigh lightly on your skin and no longer make it crawl. And the ego says that you are insane and your only hope is to go back to the way that you were before. And you smile at its pitiful gasp.

Who could reject the Love of God and the deep peace and faith inside that everything leads to joy? Who would surrender the returning gifts that feel so good and never cease to surprise with delight? Who would want to see a reflection that is not empowering and supportive?

While I am still in the world, I will take one day at a time and work on my forgiveness lessons and open my heart to the Holy Spirit. If I do that, it is a "good" day because I moved closer to my eternal reality. There is no other "real" objective possible in the dream. It is the beginning and the end. It is the only thing that matters. Everything else is temporal and of the ego. The ego's desire to make the illusion real is nothing more than a projection of my own fear.

I work because I must support my body as I retrain my mind. In the meantime I open up to inspiration and have fun with life! I use my travels to spread joy by simply being with others. If I am successful in my endeavors, it is merely a byproduct of my surrender to my ultimate reality.

All relationships are holy because I realize in the deepest core of my being that everyone is me. I have no expectations for them, for they are already perfect. I do not need to desire that they change, for they will if that is their desire. I wait for events to conspire and inspiration to lead me to action. When it does, I again need do nothing except follow where it leads and allow it to provide.

I am guided by my intuition and sense of creativity. I recognize true inspiration because it makes me happy and content in the deepest core of my being.

This book is priming the pump of your inner (and maybe even unconscious) desire to awaken from the dream that life as we know it is the only reality. It is doubtful that you would have gotten to this point if the ideas were not making sense and you were not having some success with the concepts. Maybe you are even familiar with them and this has been an exercise in reinforcement.

Waking to our true reality is accepting the fact that we are the Christ who is having a little fantasy that the universe exists and that he (we) can experience it as a being separate from God. That's what we are, a little spark of the Child of God at play. We are Brahma playing a game with Maya! That's what every-one is. That's what everything is. Everything in the physical universe and the many dimensions above and the lesser gods who pretend to be the Source are all part of this complicated illusion.

If we try to understand it, we will fail, for it is set up for failure. Working hard and trying to awaken will tend to keep us search-ing and experiencing just enough to think that enlightenment is right around the next corner. It is like trying really hard to fall asleep. The harder we try the more elusive it becomes. If we relax and surrender to the natural process of falling asleep it happens quickly. Waking is surrender to a natural ability that everyone has.

At the end of the search all realize the fact that there is only One, and that is God. Nothing else exists. The Christ that you are is God. We need not search. We are already home. We never left. We just forgot.

> We share one life because we have one Source, a Source from which perfection comes to us, remaining always in the holy minds which He created perfect. As we were, so are we now and will forever be. A sleeping mind must waken, as it sees its own perfection mirroring the Lord of life so perfectly it fades into what is reflected there. And now it is no more a mere reflection. It becomes the thing reflected, and

> the light which makes reflection possible. No vision now is needed. For the wakened mind is one that knows its Source, its Self, its Holiness.
>
> —*A Course in Miracles* W167.12.1–7

This is not a concept that people grasp easily. There is heavy resistance. It can be a fear-filled idea as the small self thinks that its existence is meaningless because it is not "real." The mind may imagine being swallowed into some greater whole and losing its unique identity as an individual, which is sacred to our way of thinking. People imagine a cosmic Borg conquering and assimilating them into a zombie-filled collective and subjugating their desires to its own. It is one of our greatest fears.

The irony is that we have already been assimilated and indoctrinated into a way of thinking, and we are living it all day every day. We don't notice because it is widely accepted and supported at every turn. This doesn't make it true. We are merely unaware. When we become aware of the possibility of a different reality we are, of course, afraid of it. It is fear that keeps us from realizing that the greatest gift in all eternity is to remember our magnificence and be given the opportunity to surrender to it.

> To ease the transition of identification from self to Self, it is helpful to know that the lesser becomes replaced by the greater, and thus, no loss is experienced. The comfort and security that was gleaned from clinging to one's identification with the small self is miniscule compared to the discovery of the true Self. The Self is much closer to the feeling of "Me." The little "me" had all kinds of failings, fears, and sufferings. The real "Me" is beyond all such possibility. The little "me" had to carry the burden of the fear of death, whereas the real "Me" is immortal and beyond all time and space. Gratification at the transition is complete and total. The relief that all one's lifetimes of fears were groundless and imaginary is so enormous that for a period of time it is very difficult to even function in the

> world. With the reprieve from the death sentence, the wondrous gift of Life springs forth now in its full splendor, unclouded by anxiety or the pressure of time. With the cessation of time, the doors swing open to an eternal joy; the love of God becomes the Reality. The Knowingness of the Truth of all Life and Existence stands forth with stunning Self-revelation. The wonderment of God is so all encompassing and enormous that it surpasses all possible imagination. To be at last truly and finally home is profound in the totality of its completeness. The idea that man fears God then seems so ludicrous that it is a tragic insanity.
>
> —David Hawkins, *Eye of the I,* p 87

When you begin to question your deepest beliefs and search for meaning outside of the generally accepted orthodox principles, you are opening up to an inner knowing that has always been there. It is the desire to wake up to your true reality because the one you are living is not filling the deep void and you can ignore that void no more.

There are many things that can spark this desire. Despair and depression are conditions that may cause us to begin the search. Great loss is another one. Other times it can be ignited by great art or the beauty of nature. Great love can push one to reach still further. Meditation can open heretofore unknown pathways to understanding. Whatever the genesis, this yearning can grow. It is innate within all of us, it is our heritage and we can postpone, but never avoid it.

Once begun the search yields results in the form that suits our requirements best at that moment in our lives. The result may be a conversation or a realization or a book or something else that meets the need. Our thoughts create events in our lives because we are the dreamer manifesting everything, even our own discomfort. As we learned previously the unconscious mind is the real driver, causing things to manifest in our lives whether we plan them or not. That is why strong emotions are such powerful generators. Strong emotions affect our subconscious desires. Weak emotions do not. Conscious desires are weak compared to unconscious ones.

Once sparked, the desire to wake can also be manifested. The concepts are not that difficult. Our resistance to them is the hard part. That is why we must retrain our mind with the ideas reviewed here. If the goal is to awaken, it will happen. This goal is rarely the starting point. It usually arrives after one applies thoughts like those mentioned in this book to their daily trials. This results in positive changes, thus proving (to yourself) that there is a reality operating in life that is not understood by most. The question of what it is and why it exists leads only one place: enlightenment. Enlightenment is just a fancy word for waking up to your true reality. The question of why is central. Without an understanding of why we have the ability achieve peace, joy and love, why we are able to manifest our desires, why we receive what we give, why we can tap into inspiration and why we are resistant to doing these things, we will not be able to move into this stage of development.

We can be the most peaceful, loving, giving, surrendering, non-judgmental people ever born, but if we think that the physical world is our true reality then we will miss the opportunity to move beyond it and unite with our ultimate reality as one with God.

This is why we use the world as a classroom to practice our forgiveness lessons. We are not predisposed to move beyond worldly ideals. We have a lifetime of habituated thinking to overcome, and we have our ego resisting us every step of the way. Neither of these obstacles is insurmountable. To a truly desirous person, they are gifts without which the goal could not be reached. Practice does "make perfect" our understanding, and with help and guidance, which is always forthcoming if we truly want it, our progress will be remarkable if not inspiring.

The path up out of the dream is not linear, and there is no formula that will accomplish the task. Although we are one in a cosmic sense, in the worldly sense we must make our own decision and find our own way. Even after we have woken up, we will find that we slip back and are enjoying or combating our daily existence. This is okay. We cannot function in physical space without some attachment to, and belief in, its reality. We are learning a new way of thinking. It can help our "life" immeasurably, and it can lead us to our destiny if we let it.

Seeking can develop into an end in itself, and this is yet another impediment to taking the final step into ultimate surrender. There is always another spiritual subject to learn and another process to perfect. This search is unending and leads in circles. It is an ego trap, of course. Once the idea has manifested in your life that you are one with God and all that is and your purpose is to internalize this idea in the deepest core of your being, then you have found the answer. Searching beyond this is counterproductive. You have found the reality you sought. Embracing it is your next step, not more searching.

Adyashanti sums it up in a wonderful metaphor. He says that "spirituality" is a drug that cures the sickness of wanting to wake up in the same way that antibiotics cure an infection in the body. Once the antibiotics have cured our disease, we stop taking them because we are no longer sick. Spiritual students on the other hand sometimes want to continue taking "spirituality" even after it has provided its benefits. They have subconsciously replaced the goal with the process and in so doing lost sight of their objective.

Waking up is like discovering that you have an ability to fly that you never knew about before. It makes you laugh with joy as you learn to control your flight. Your perspective rises, and your vision becomes clear and deep. You are an eagle who can see a mouse from a mile high! You discover that you can float on updrafts of peace toward Love, and even though you see the mouse, you aren't hungry for mice anymore. You are drinking from the eternal fountain, and it is so much more satisfying.

Chapter 25

Implications and Suggestions

She generally gave herself good advice
(though she very seldom followed it).
—Alice's Adventures in Wonderland

If you experienced an excitement as you read and understood the ideas in this book, and if you feel that you have actually touched a part of your being that you did not know existed and it has become real for you, then this work has achieved its objective.

You are on the road to deep self-discovery, and it can profoundly affect your life from this moment forward if you let it. The journey is not over; indeed, it has just begun. The reality that you glimpsed is already fading and will soon return from whence it came if you do not cherish it and keep a flame burning to lead you onward.

The ego is a wily rascal and is merely biding time waiting for the moment when it can turn your attention back to the world of form. Your attention will turn back, for it must in order for you to complete the journey. But it need never be as it was before you learned of your eternal reality.

If you practice the ideas we have reviewed, forgive yourself for lapses, ask for help to learn the lessons you came to learn, and do this every day, if only for a short time, you will continue to move forward. If you can practice more than that, your journey will be more rewarding and you will start to experience the joy that arises from peace and leads to Love.

The ego will tempt you, but you have the will to overlook that temptation most of the time and the ability to not feel guilty when you don't. Over time your capacity to consciously restrain your ego with compassion, forgiveness and release will become habit, and soon your ego will stop having so much of an effect on you.

Judgmental thoughts will provide wonderful material for your forgiveness exercises for many years to come, and as such will produce joy in the accomplishment because you know that you have taken yet another step forward. Each step brings you closer and makes the next one easier. Instead of tiring, you get stronger as you go because the rewards are so tangible in feelings of happiness and serenity. Your smile becomes a fixture as you spontaneously laugh at the both the smallest joys and the biggest problems in your life. You can become tuned to your Higher Self and allow it to consciously experience your life with you as you listen to its guidance and act accordingly.

Re-reading critical concepts like the chapters in this book on Resistance, Giving and Receiving, Judgment and The Mirror will help you to see them in action every day. Your relationships will only benefit from embracing the idea that everyone is a reflection of you. Your relationships with others are the key to forward progress (because they are you), and as you work to make them holy, by embracing the ideas herein, you will transform yourself and everyone you meet. As you let go of your attachment to outcomes, you can open to trust that everything is moving together to produce the best result for all concerned. Even if that result is painful, you will know that it is merely pointing the way forward. Acceptance will surely follow your understanding of this fact.

Strong thoughts and feelings are the most powerful force in the universe, and we can gain control over them. Remind yourself every day that you are the Son or Daughter of God, the Christ consciousness, the Dreamer and the Author. Look on the world as a classroom and practice your lessons, for you are training your mind to think differently as you accomplish them. You are using your conscious mind to retrain you subconscious mind, and it will learn, too, with time and practice. You will see the results of your efforts every day as positive outcomes manifest around you, and opportunities you hardly dared to dream become reality.

Feelings of accomplishment will be replaced with humility. You will realize that you are experiencing "earthly rewards" because they are the result of moving forward on your eternal path. Your need to learn painful lessons will diminish, and abundance will arrive, although you may find that your definition of it has changed. You are walking forward on the path to embracing your destiny, and you do not need extravagance or power or admiration anymore.

You might need a new house or a new car or money for school, and a promotion at work or a new job or successful investments will provide for your needs. It may provide far more than you need, and you might wonder why you are the recipient of these gifts. Your desire to use them in an orgy of earthly delights will not exist, nor will a desire to hoard them, and this will be a clue that you have made real progress.

Negative outcomes and events are opportunities to forgive and thus reduce the need for them to recur in your life. In this way they can be perceived as beneficial and joyfully embraced until they are needed no longer.

Keep studying the path. Keep learning the lessons of those who are teaching truth, but do not make the process the goal. Wake up every day to your classroom of lessons in your eternal reality and realize that it begins and ends inside of you. True spiritual growth is an internal process, and using it for anything more than achieving peace, happiness and Love drawn from the eternal makes the illusion real and strengthens the ego. Engage in activities that help others move forward, but do not shout the message from the rooftops. Those who are interested in learning will find you and give you the opportunity to share from a place of inspiration.

Writing this book has been my way of internalizing the instruction I have received. It is an exercise in embracing truth and developing trust. I have experienced the rewards to a degree that propels me forward, and I realize that although I may have shortened the journey I am still traveling the pathway home. If these writings have found their way into your hands and made their way into your heart, you can rest assured that it was no accident and you are ready for them. If you were not, this "unknown" would not have become known to you.

Namasté and happy travels!

Robert Shay
2009

www.peacejoyandlove.com

Appendix A

A Course in Miracles

Workbook Lesson 152

The power of decision is my own.

The power of decision is my own.

No one can suffer loss unless it be his own decision. No one suffers pain except his choice elects this state for him. No one can grieve nor fear nor think him sick unless these are the outcomes that he wants. And no one dies without his own consent. Nothing occurs but represents your wish, and nothing is omitted that you choose. Here is your world, complete in all details. Here is its whole reality for you. And it is only here salvation is.

You may believe that this position is extreme, and too inclusive to be true. Yet can truth have exceptions? If you have the gift of everything, can loss be real? Can pain be part of peace, or grief of joy? Can fear and sickness enter in a mind where love and perfect holiness abide? Truth must be all-inclusive, if it be the truth at all. Accept no opposites and no exceptions, for to do so is to contradict the truth entirely.

Salvation is the recognition that the truth is true, and nothing else is true. This you have heard before, but may not yet accept both parts of it. Without the first, the second has no meaning. But without the second, is the first no longer true. Truth cannot have an opposite. This cannot be too often said and thought about. For if what is not true is true as well as what is true, then part of truth is false. And truth has lost its meaning. Nothing but the truth is true, and what is false is false.

This is the simplest of distinctions, yet the most obscure. But not because it is a difficult distinction to perceive. It is concealed behind a vast array of choices that do not appear to be entirely your own. And thus the truth appears to have some aspects that belie consistency, but do not seem to be but contradictions introduced by you.

As God created you, you must remain unchangeable, with transitory states by definition false. And that includes all shifts in feeling, alterations in conditions of the body and the mind; in all awareness and in all response. This is the all-inclusiveness which sets the truth apart from falsehood, and the false kept separate from the truth, as what it is.

Is it not strange that you believe to think you made the world you see is arrogance? God made it not. Of this you can be sure. What can He know of the ephemeral, the sinful and the guilty, the afraid, the suffering and lonely, and the mind that lives within a body that must die? You but accuse Him of insanity, to think He made a world where such things seem to have reality. He is not mad. Yet only madness makes a world like this.

To think that God made chaos, contradicts His Will, invented opposites to truth, and suffers death to triumph over life; all this is arrogance. Humility would see at once these things are not of Him. And can you see what God created not? To think you can is merely to believe you can perceive what God willed not to be. And what could be more arrogant than this?

Let us today be truly humble, and accept what we have made as what it is. The power of decision is our own. Decide but to accept your rightful place as co-creator of the universe, and all you think you made will disappear. What rises to awareness then will be all that there ever was, eternally as it is now. And it will take the place of self-deceptions made but to usurp the altar to the Father and the Son.

Today we practice true humility, abandoning the false pretense by which the ego seeks to prove it arrogant. Only the ego can be arrogant. But truth is humble in acknowledging its mightiness, its changelessness and its eternal wholeness, all-encompassing, God's perfect gift to His beloved Son. We lay aside the arrogance which says that we are sinners, guilty and afraid, ashamed of what we are; and lift our hearts in true humility instead to Him Who has created us immaculate, like to Himself in power and in love.

The power of decision is our own. And we accept of Him that which we are, and humbly recognize the Son of God. To recognize God's Son implies as well that all self-concepts have been laid aside, and recognized as false. Their arrogance has been perceived. And in humility the radiance of God's Son, his gentleness, his perfect sinlessness, his Father's Love, his right to Heaven and release from hell, are joyously accepted as our own.

Now do we join in glad acknowledgment that lies are false, and only truth is true. We think of truth alone as we arise, and spend five minutes practicing its ways, encouraging our frightened minds with this:

The power of decision is my own.
This day I will accept myself as what
my Father's Will created me to be.

Then will we wait in silence, giving up all self-deceptions, as we humbly ask our Self that He reveal Himself to us. And He

Who never left will come again to our awareness, grateful to restore His home to God, as it was meant to be.

In patience wait for Him throughout the day, and hourly invite Him with the words with which the day began, concluding it with this same invitation to your Self. God's Voice will answer, for He speaks for you and for your Father. He will substitute the peace of God for all your frantic thoughts, the truth of God for self-deceptions, and God's Son for your illusions of yourself.

Appendix B

Blogs provide a forum for those who chose to share their understanding and discuss spiritual topics. Some are quite profound and awake in their content. An example.

NISARGADATTA'S MESSAGE

http://nisargadattasmessage.blogspot.com/

Posted by Gilbert Schultz
June 21, 2008

Is there anything to know, anywhere to go, anything to do? – The answer is, no, there is not. –There is just this ever present being which is always and ever whole or complete in itself, what is referred to in Advaita as One without a second. –If there is no second or other to this being that you already are right here and now, who then is the separate person with destiny and free will that you presently and mistakenly take to be your identity?

Look into this for yourself and solve this riddle of apparent separation or sin, as it is referred to in some of the religious traditions. Are you separate, are you a miserable sinner or a virtuous saint? – Perhaps you are neither? Are you separate from the animating life force, or what we refer to as consciousness? Is consciousness personal (yours or mine) or is it universal? I think it is rather obvious that consciousness, sentience, nature or life itself is universal and isn't the property of any person or individual.

No separate person or individual has control over life and death, so called. Life has us, we as these seeming separate entities, don't have it. That means that we as these phenomenal objects, humans, animals, nature in general, are being lived or animated by this utterly impersonal life force or universal consciousness. If this fact is realized, it results in freedom from this bondage of self, this phantom entity "me" that we had been shoring up, protecting, and investing all of our energy into.

This frees everything up and life or living becomes an effortless, endless flow of pure functioning without beginning or ending – a timeless throb (Sphurana) of pure presence awareness. This infinite vibration, this ever fresh, ever new, ceaseless I. I, this unbroken and formless I that is always and ever present, pure functioning, cognizing emptiness, is what you truly 'are'. THIS is nothing to the mind and that is why it is constantly being ignored. THIS that is being pointed to is nothing perceivable or conceivable. THIS emptiness suffused with awareness, this aware no thing cannot be understood or grasped by the mind of the so called individual simply because the mind as such is a thing, a bundle of memories, past experiences and concepts and it does not want to know or be introduced to this aware no thing which is the actual non dual Absolute or reality that alone can resolve or solve all problems and bring about genuine liberation and spiritual satisfaction.

The reason why the mind doesn't want to know about what is being pointed to here is that it will loose it's illusory power and will no longer be running the show as it had always mistakenly assumed itself to be doing. No "me", no problem! All problems are problems of relationship – "me" and the so called other, but if there is no me there with any substance or independent nature of it's own, then how can there be any problems? The simple answer is – there can't be!

THIS all-knowing presence awareness is no thing to the mind or the so called "me" of memory. This reference point, this acquired me of dead memories, concepts and past experiences is invalid; it doesn't exist when it is fearlessly looked into. So when I say I like this or I don't like something else, what is this 'I' that I am talking about? Isn't it just a dead image, a concept given by your parents and society to which you then added all the past events and experiences of your made up life story?

Have a good look at it, don't just go off half baked, don't run back into the mind of dead language and acquired thoughts, learning and concepts and say, yes, but what about this and what about my bad childhood etc, etc? That's just a cop out, a load of make belief and untruth, because in truth nothing has happened at all. THIS self-shining, non dual pure knowing awareness has never ever changed or been affected by anything; it's undeniable, intangible presence is enabling you to read these words here and now. You have never left this all knowing awareness. THIS is THAT non dual Absolute – The TRUTH that makes you free, but do you want the TRUTH or do you prefer the lie of limitation (birth and death) and separation (sin)?– End.

What is my true position? Where am I actually located? Isn't it a fact that I exist in and as space itself? Does space have any centre or circumference? For anything to exist it would have to be in space, and space itself is nothing, it has no location and is all pervasive.

Everything arises and is finally subsumed in that sky like space. This space that you are seeing right in front of you is indestructible and invulnerable because it has no dimensions and is nothing or no thing. Things perish, but the space that they are appearing in is imperishable – vast emptiness that wasn't created by anyone or anything.

This space-like awareness which expresses through the mind as the thought "I am" is formless. The basis of this knowledge "I am" is unborn empty-awareness-knowing-ness. True knowledge (Janna) has no shape or form. I am THAT by which I know I am. I am infinitely and eternally without any shape or form; nothing can touch me or know me because I alone Am – One without a second. THIS activity of knowing, the knowledge "I am", doesn't have any shape, form, or design. Trace any thought back to its origin, there you have all the love, all the power, all the knowledge and abundance you can ever need. Eg: you are! Always and ever.

Realize that what you are seeking – perfection – you already are. The concept or thought "I am' is the news spontaneously announcing your true condition or natural state of perfection, which in fact, you have never left. Have a look at that – I am is not I was (past) or I will be (future), but I am here and now Absolutely and eternally – before Abraham was I am. A step closer – before Jesus Christ was I am. I am always and ever, and so are you. I am THAT, you are THAT, there is nothing now or ever that is not THAT. Isn't this clear and obvious to no one by now?

You know 'you are'. That is the teaching in a nutshell. Has anyone ever left that pure being-ness (Sat)? Can anyone negate their being-ness? It is quite obvious that they cannot. However Being-ness or the non dual Absolute cannot know itself objectively – That which is seeking is that which is sought. Objectively it's not there. That's why you will never find the answer you are seeking in the mind, because you cannot find something that you have never lost – your own Being, your true identity – I am.

You are not what you have taken yourself to be – this corpse like physical body and it's illusory mind – the "me" of memory.

The past is dead and never really happened, so who are you? What do you hope to achieve? From where have you come and to where are you proceeding? Ask these questions of yourself and the vice-like grip of the illusory self-centre will loose its hold on you and fall away without any effort on your part, leaving you here and now, Omnipresent, awake, and aware as you have always been.

You have never left this presence awareness except in conceptual speculation and memory. Even then when the past is being recalled or the future is being anticipated, this is only happening presently. You never actually go to the future or return to the past except in conceptual thinking (mind). You can never live in the past or future, you can only live presently. The past is dead and the future has not yet arrived.

When the future arrives it will be presently – NOW. This is the only instant there ever is, there is no other time but now no matter what position the hands of the clock are in, and every instant is the best instant, the first instant of knowing, ever fresh, ever new, uncontaminated by any imagination

The Omnipresent, unchanging equal-ness of this space like activity of pure knowing is Advaita. This knowing has nothing to do with the knowing of the mind which is time, past and future, knowing facts like this or that, he or she, the duality of phenomena. No one can negate this presence of awareness nor can it be grasped with a thought or concept. Therefore it is immediately seen to be true, as it is continually pointed out and alluded to in Advaita, that you will never find the answer to the riddle of existence and non existence in the mind as such. This is all anyone, so called, needs to know.

Appendix C

Meet Me Here (Adyashanti – from *My Secret Is Silence***)**

Join me here Now
where there are no points of view.
Slip under good and bad
right and wrong
worthy and unworthy
sinner and saint.

Meet me here
where everything is unframed
before understanding
and not understanding.

Meet me here
where silence roars
where stillness is dancing
where the eternal is living and dying.

Meet me here
where you are not you
where you are It
and It is unspeakable.

Meet me here
where all points of view
merge into a single point
that then disappears.

Meet me here
before there ever was something
before there ever was nothing.

Meet me here
where everything speaks of this
where everything has
always spoken this
where nothing is ever lost or found.

Meet me here.

Appendix D

From: Absence From Felicity The Story of Helen Schucman and Her Scribing of A Course In Miracles, By Kenneth Wapnick pp. 50 – 52.

The Gentleman

The first dream we consider is "The Gentleman" where Helen is confronted by a Gentleman, symbolic of Jesus, hence the capital "G." He offers Helen the choice of joining his world, which among other things has an "economy of great abundance" and "is not an economy of scarcity", its inhabitants have no needs of any kind. The Gentleman is totally non-confrontive, and exerts no coercion on Helen at all. He merely states the reality of Helen's choice, and allows her total freedom to accept or refuse his offer. Characteristically, Helen is uncommitted, and still retains the right to choose her own personal world: "'Thank you for the invitation.'... I haven't made up my mind about coming, but if I do, I'll insist on bringing my own slack suits." This is the dream:

> "Wouldn't it be wonderful if it would stay like this all year round?" I say to myself, slipping back my cape and baking happily in the hot sun. "But of course it won't. In just a little while it'll be winter and the snow and cold will come back and I'll freeze to death again. It'll stay like that for months and months, and I'll get colder and colder. I've lived through a lot of winters, but somehow I have a feeling that I won't get through another one." I begin to shiver in spite of the heat, and pull my cape closely around my shoulders.
> "Perhaps you'd like to spend the winter underground with us this year?" asks the Gentleman. We are standing in an enormous underground cavern, lit by hundreds of small crystal clusters of lights set in the high, arched ceiling. The lights are so remote that they seem like stars, and the high dome suggests the open sky....

"This place is surely intended for a great many people," I say. "Where is everybody?"
"They haven't come as yet," the Gentleman explains, "but they will. There is no need for them to come here as long as it's still summer. And now tell me," he asks, returning to his first question, "how would you like to spend the winter underground with us?"
"I don't quite know," I say, uneasily. "I'd better think it over first.... I'm afraid I'd be dreadfully uncomfortable here."
"You needn't worry about that," says the Gentleman, reassuringly. "You'll be quite safe here...."
"It's not that I doubt your word, of course," I add, hastily.
The Gentleman laughs pleasantly. "It's quite evident that you do doubt my word," he says, "but it's not likely that you could take anybody's word for anything. Faith isn't one of your strong points, now, is it?..."
"How's the weather here?" I ask next, feeling that this is a really important question for me.
"It's quite warm and very pleasant," says the Gentleman. "In fact, most people come here at first because of the climate. If they decide to stay, though, and most of them do, they usually do so for better reasons."
"Such as?" I ask, curiously.
"That's hard to explain," says the Gentleman. "It's quite different here; so different that it's hard to get used to at first. You see, the environment itself is perfect, but what you make of it is strictly your own affair. That in itself makes a great difference. But understanding the difference depends on your ability to perceive it, which, of course, nobody can do for you. You may not be able to see any difference at all, which would be most unfortunate. I've been hoping you'll learn in time. But if not, you can always go away. Nobody will detain you."
So far it sounds fair enough to me. However, there are still some further questions to be settled.
"What does one wear down here?" I ask, mentally reviewing my wardrobe.
"You don't have to be concerned with that," answers the Gentleman. "We take care of all such details for you." He leads me into one of the shops. In the open show-cases are piles of curious-looking black slack-suits....
The slack-suits don't particularly appeal to me. However, I examine them, chiefly to be polite.
"How many would I need?" I ask.

"Oh, you won't need more than one," says the Gentleman.
I don't like this at all. One would hardly be enough. I begin at once to figure out some way of getting more, and decide that, since the show-cases are open, it would be easy to steal an extra suit or two without being discovered. As if I had spoken out loud the Gentleman answers, still pleasantly and without criticism, "I told you it was different here. It's quite impossible to steal anything. Ours is not an economy of scarcity. We have plenty of everything. You just take it if you want it. As for the suits, I didn't say you could have only one. I said you'd need only one. You can have as many as you want.... ours is not a money economy. There is nothing you can either steal or buy. We have an economy of great abundance, because where there is scarcity it is very difficult for people to realize that there is nothing worth stealing or buying. You'd better start off by taking as many of everything as you see fit. After a while it will no longer occur to you to take more than you need. There just won't be any sense in doing it."
I am inclined to doubt this, but refrain from saying so. "I have two very pretty blue slack-suits at home," I say. "Do you think it would be wrong to bring them with me?"
"Certainly not," the Gentleman says. "How can it be wrong, if you think they'll make you happier? You won't wear them very long, though."...
I am beginning to feel confused. Obviously the Gentleman was right. This place is very different, and I'm not too sure that I'd get along here very well. I've got by in my own world, after a fashion, but this place might be something I couldn't cope with.
"If you don't care about appearances, and if people can't steal or buy anything, how do you manage to get along?" I ask. "I mean, how does one get to be noticed or liked?"
"That's very simple," says the Gentleman. "If you're nice, people will notice you and like you. If not, why then, they won't. It will take a long time for you to be either noticed or liked. You may, in fact, be very nearly invisible to the people here for quite a while, because what you emphasize they won't even see. But still, since you can't stand another cold winter, you can't lose anything by taking a chance. If you like you can regard it as an experiment. You can always go away. It's still summer, so you have plenty of time to think it over. The decision isn't final, either way, so don't get a notion that it's a life and death affair. It really isn't. When the fall comes, see how you feel about it, and then do whatever you like."

> We shake hands. "Thank you for the invitation," I say, politely, and go out. I haven't made up my mind about coming, but if I do, I'll insist on bringing my own slack-suits. I don't believe in Utopias....

Again, the final lines reflect, as does the whole dream, the part of Helen's mind that resisted Jesus' offer to enter his world of abundance and peace, referred to in *A Course in Miracles* as the real world. To the end, Helen retained her right to choose to remain exactly where she was, even though she was clearly not happy.

Additional Reading

A Course in Miracles
Foundation for Inner Peace

Power vs. Force
David Hawkins

Eye of the I
David Hawkins

Many Lives Many Masters
Brian Weiss

Journey of Souls
Michael Newton

I Am That
Sri Nisargadatta Maharaj

Your Life
Bruce McArthur

Letters From the After Life
Elsa Barker

Ask and It Is Given
Ester and Jerry Hicks

The Relationship Handbook
George Pransky

Absence From Felicity
Kenneth Wapnick

How to Meditate
Lawrence LeShan

Excuse Me! Your Life Is Waiting
Lynn Grabhorn

Inner Peace
Paramahansa Yogananda

Take Me to Truth
Nouk Sanchez and Thomas Viera

The Way of the Superior Man
David Deida

The Power of Now
Eckhart Tolle

A New Earth
Eckhart Tolle

Spontaneous Awakenings
(CD Set)
Adyashanti

Silence of the Heart
Robert Adams

Wake Up Now
Stephan Bodian

The Disappearance of the Universe
Gary Renard

Soul Visioning
Susan Wisehart

The Mastery of Love
Don Miguel Ruiz

Made in the USA